THE BOOK
OF THE
ROYAL WEDDING

THE BOOK
OF THE
ROYAL WEDDING

ALASTAIR BURNET

SUMMIT BOOKS
New York

The publishers would like to thank Major and Mrs Ronald Ferguson, and Miss Sarah Ferguson's Nanny, Ritva Risu for their generous contribution to this book.

Interviews and research by Andrew Morton

Published by Summit Books
A Division of Simon & Schuster, Inc.
Simon & Schuster Building, Rockefeller Center,
1230 Avenue of the Americas, New York, New York 10020
SUMMIT BOOKS and colophon are registered trademarks of
Simon & Schuster, Inc.

Designed by Martin Bristow
Edited by Fiona Holman and Sarah Coombe
Picture research by Sarah Coombe

.

Video film processed by BPCC Video Graphics
Typeset by SX Composing Limited
Printed and bound by Printer Industria Gráfica SA, Barcelona, Spain
D.L. B. 26576-1986

*Half title: A charming photograph of Prince Andrew and Miss Sarah Ferguson
taken by Gene Nocon shortly after the engagement.*

*Frontispiece: A formal photograph of Prince Andrew and Miss Ferguson
in the Blue Drawing-room at Buckingham Palace.*

*Facing page: Prince Andrew and Miss Ferguson on the balcony at Buckingham Palace
when they accompanied the Queen during the celebrations
for her sixtieth birthday in April.*

CONTENTS

A ROYAL ENGAGEMENT

PRINCE Andrew and his bride can never be 'the young people next door'. Yet no one who saw them on their wedding day sees them now as being in any way close to the crown in the years ahead: that role belongs to another branch of the family. Their own children will be expected, as they may readily prefer, to live lives of their own that are increasingly less royal, as Princess Anne's two children undoubtedly will. Yet there always will be an aura about them, the Queen's second son and his wife, that is as unlikely to diminish just as popular interest in them is unlikely to diminish. The interest in the couple is not in the succession to the throne, as it was internationally at the wedding of the Prince and Princess of Wales, it is in themselves, and in what they make of their lives in the years ahead. Their marriage is an important one in helping to decide what priorities the Queen's own family will follow in a new generation that has a freedom of choice that preceding ones were not given, or did not give themselves.

The marriage, like those of the Queen's two older children, has ended the idea of dynastic marriage in the family, and, like the Prince of Wales's, opened the door to marriage within the court, to children of courtiers. This is something new. No one could imagine the children of George V's courtiers being accepted in the immediate family; and when Princess Margaret thought of it for herself she was weightily dissuaded. What has made it different for the daughters of the Earl Spencer and now Major Ronald Ferguson is that the world both inside and outside the court has changed out of all recognition since the 1950s in its expectations and its ways.

It does not hinder the course of true love in the House of Windsor if the parents of the prospective brides or bridegrooms are known to the family, and themselves know what is expected by the family, or if the children have been part of the circle from time to time, and so know, too, what is expected of them. It is no hindrance, either, if there is a direct relationship with the royal family, however distant or tenuous. So it is an

On page 6: Behind the stiff formality of the engagement announcement lay a romance that delighted the couple's families and friends as well as the nation.

On page 7: Engagement day and the moment the photographers had been waiting for. During the photo-call in the grounds of Buckingham Palace Miss Ferguson delighted the photographers by kissing her fiancé firmly on the cheek.

attribute of the Ferguson family that its genealogy goes back (unlike the Queen's own) directly to Charles II, or that Major Ferguson himself is a first cousin of Princess Alice, Duchess of Gloucester, the widow of one of the Queen's uncles. But what is plainly more important nowadays than ancestry is that the newcomers to the family should bring with them an awareness of the everyday world that they know which none of the Queen's own children, however hard they try, can ever quite know.

Before her marriage, while being on the edge of the royal circle without ever being quite in it, Princess Andrew gained an experience of a broader part of society (though not of the broadest) by which to judge better for herself what the hopes, the interests and the problems of at least a range of people, especially other young people, may be. She has worked, if not always exactly for a living, then to help her live within her means. She knows what it is to travel on public transport. She knows what it is to make up her mind without advisor or escort. She knows, above all, what it is to be unknown in a crowd. This will all matter, just as the views of her ally and friend the Princess of Wales will matter, in the adaptation of the family they have both joined.

The Prince and Princess are cheerful enough, confident enough, ebullient enough to make their own way in the world as royal people, to

A charming photograph of Sarah, aged three and a half, taken by Lord Lichfield, the Queen's cousin and long-established society photographer. The Fergusons' Finnish nanny recalls that Sarah was 'something of a tomboy at this age' and was always full of mischief.

use their own liking for people to further the causes they wish to help, and to tread chiefly, if not only, on the toes they really want to tread on. What may be indicative, though, for them and for other members of the family, is if and how they can reconcile their own wishes to continue at what they know as work, he in the navy and she in publishing, with the inhibitions that being in even an enlightened royal family has usually imposed. They are independently-minded young people. They may need to be.

It is greatly to the credit of the junior members of the royal family, especially the Gloucesters, the Kents, Princess Alexandra and, not least, Princess Anne, that they have adopted their own good causes and charities and have worked assiduously, and often anonymously, for them. They have altered impressively both the duties and the public perception of what was once the foundation-stone laying, tree-planting monarchy of which the Duke of Windsor grew so bored. It is now a question of if the expectations of the modern, democratic monarchy will let them take that adaptation further.

The present public expectation of monarchy is, as it has been since Queen Victoria's day, of one that is desirable and useful, but is the more interesting because it is a family. To the undeferential the emergence of a

A birthday photograph of Prince Andrew aged six, taken in the grounds of Buckingham Palace. He was by now a boisterous and extrovert boy, delighting and exasperating his family and the Palace staff alike.

new member of the family into the limelight is as unimportant as to
many of the deferential it is as important as the casting of a new actress in
a television serial. That does not materially touch the estimation of the
Queen herself; as she grows older, older for the first time than her prime
ministers will be and with the experience that goes with age, the respect
for her is bound to heighten. It is with the young, in Britain, the
Commonwealth, the United States and Europe, that the royal family's
next concern has to be. That is where the Prince and Princess may well
be instrumental in their idea of, and influence on, what a working
monarchy should mean.

What they have given television and the world so far is high hopes,
a day of promise, a day to remember; even (since the politicians forbade
it) a holiday for the independently-minded who watched it. Royal
weddings have come out of obscurity in the twentieth century, to the
increasing diversion and enjoyment of millions. They are the more fun
when the people taking part are evidently enjoying it all themselves. It is
a marriage that has begun well.

THE BRIDEGROOM

PRINCE Andrew is a good-looking young man, better looking than his brothers, though a distance from being the Robert Redford the Prince of Wales compares him with. He smiles readily and well, and to public effect, and he has good teeth to show. He looks good in uniform and he has kept his hair. The Prince has a good war record behind him in the Falklands, and a highly competent service reputation since. He is capital with people and crowds, knowing what they like, and the royal occasions he has time for he does to everyone's, well almost everyone's, satisfaction.

Prince Andrew is the Queen's second son, the one that destiny has not offered, and is now wholly unlikely to offer, a prospect of the crown (as it did to second sons in two of his three preceding royal generations). His elder brother, the Prince of Wales, already has two sons. So, now, Prince Andrew's marriage is not ringed about with expectations of greatness, nor even of enforced prominence. If he is to live out his life, as his grandfather and great-grandfather once expected to live out theirs (and his father might have hoped to have been given more time to do in his) as a naval officer first and foremost, neither he nor his wife may feel any particular sense of disappointment. They may even feel a distinct sense of relief. But he is a character, and one that is likely to be around, and not out of the public eye, for a long time to come.

He happens to be someone about whom it is very easy to have two or even more views. There is the Prince to whom young women have flocked uninvited but not always unrewarded. There is the Prince who is his father's son with up-to-date ideas but apparently uncaring of sensibilities or reputations. There is the Prince who has felt let down by his women friends and acquaintances and who has been lonely and vulnerable. There is the Prince who has the chance now to turn from being what people expect him to be to being what he wants to be.

On page 12: A formal photograph of Prince Andrew commissioned to mark his engagement. The Prince is wearing the ceremonial day dress of a naval lieutenant. His two medals are (right) the Jubilee medal and the South Atlantic medal with a rosette which denotes having served in the Total Exclusion Zone in the 1982 Falklands Campaign.

On page 13: The Queen commissioned Cecil Beaton, the leading royal photographer of his day, to take the first official photographs of the month-old baby Prince in the Blue Drawing-room at Buckingham Palace. According to Beaton, the baby behaved himself and 'sometimes opened its eyes'.

Prince Andrew, like his sister Princess Anne, was not given the chance to grow up decorously or demurely. So his marriage, like hers, will not be scrutinized with particular sympathy by the people who make their living writing about royal marriages. That is, once the royal honeymoon is happily past. It has been in his nature to be extrovert, and a successful career at his school, Gordonstoun, and in his profession, a helicopter pilot, has not, of itself, helped to develop the particular qualities that both his brothers exemplify in the royal family. But his own qualities, his robustness, even his escapades which mothers, at least, might have frowned on, have made him popular. People like him. They have also helped, at least, to keep the popular press popular too. It will not readily let him escape to the unexceptional life of a married naval officer.

Like his sister, Prince Andrew has contributed to his stereotype. He did spray paint at press photographers in Los Angeles when he was there trying to raise money for the British Olympic team. He later denied that he had done it on purpose, but helicopter pilots are not trained to press wrong buttons, and aspiring photographers should know what damage paint can do to cameras. His mother rightly thought it politic to compensate the aggrieved, although the British colony in Los Angeles affirmed stoutly that the Prince had meant no harm, and that he had worked devotedly to raise money for the team. Prince Andrew has in his time run around with young women, as young naval officers have been known to do, and enough of these girls found it useful afterwards to

A happy family photograph taken in the garden at Clarence House in London to mark the Queen Mother's sixtieth birthday in August 1960. Prince Andrew, then nearly six months old, was 'a jolly baby' who looked exactly like his father at the same age with his ash-blond hair and deep blue eyes.

Above: The two-year-old Prince Andrew playing hide-and-seek in the nursery at Buckingham Palace. An engaging child, he was a firm favourite of both his grandmothers who doted on him when his parents were away as they frequently were.

Left: The young Prince in the nursery at Buckingham Palace. The Queen delighted in being a mother again after a gap of ten years and spent as much time as possible with Prince Andrew. Regular visitors to the Queen's study soon became used to the sight of the little boy playing with his toys on the floor while the Queen dealt with her State papers at her desk.

Above left: A royal wave from Prince Andrew, aged four, on his way from London to join a family holiday. The young prince's sheltered and private world followed a regular routine. The weeks were spent in London at Buckingham Palace, the weekends at Windsor Castle and large family gatherings took place at Balmoral in the late summer and at Sandringham during Christmas and the New Year.

Above right: Prince Andrew watching Trooping the Colour from an upstairs window of Buckingham Palace. The Queen's two youngest children were rarely seen in public, a deliberate policy by the Queen and Prince Philip to ensure an informal upbringing away from the glare and strain of publicity.

Facing page: A photograph taken at Windsor Castle to mark the Queen's birthday in April 1962. It was at this time that the Queen gave Prince Andrew his first lessons, teaching him to count and to recite his ABC. She also gave him riding lessons in the Royal Mews on a small Shetland pony called Mr Dinkum.

advance their careers as models or actresses, or sell their stories openly to the papers – as models and actresses have been known to do. Other officers, other princes, might say they would have known better. Not all of them have.

Once there is a stereotype it is very, very hard to break. As Prince Andrew is not going to devote himself entirely to charitable work in the coming years, he will find it very hard to break his. Princess Andrew will want to help to put that right. It will be her first test.

What is not, or not yet, in the public perception is that the Prince does not need to let himself be portrayed as a selfish and self-important young man with only a wardroom wit and a well-developed Hanoverian idea of manners. Lynx helicopters are not the most sophisticated of flying machines, but not too many of his critics could fly one as he does. He got six O-levels at Gordonstoun and three A-levels, in English, history and economics. They are not the qualifications of a Hooray Henry, nor are they, indeed, the accustomed qualifications of members of his family.

In a material way, the Queen's children have grown up in a world in which the expectations of the newspaper press, and so of its readers, have become inflated about what they want to know and think of the young royals in a way that did not occur to the press about previous royal generations, or if it did occur would not have been encouraged.

Nothing deleterious was ever said about the Queen and Princess Margaret in their adolescence; there was nothing deleterious to report, but even if there had been it would have been tactfully suppressed as, in the previous generation, the behaviour of the then Prince of Wales and his youngest brother, Prince George (later the Duke of Kent), was suppressed in the 1920s and 1930s.

Facing page: Prince Andrew grew up to be a robust and sturdy little boy, as seen in this photograph taken by Cecil Beaton at Buckingham Palace in July 1964. Although a handful to look after, his nanny, Mabel Anderson was so devoted to him that she could rarely be persuaded to take her days off. The Queen's fourth child, Prince Edward was born a few months before this photograph was taken and soon joined his brother in the nursery.

Right: A family photograph taken at Frogmore to mark the Queen's birthday in April 1965. For Prince Andrew, recently turned five, the carefree nursery days had just come to an end and he had begun to have lessons in the school-room at Buckingham Palace.

Below: On the balcony of Buckingham Palace Lord Mountbatten points out to his great-nephew, Prince Andrew and his cousin, Viscount Linley the traditional RAF flypast which takes place after Trooping the Colour each June.

What happened to the Queen's children is that they emerged from the chrysalis of their schooling, in which the media observed, up to a precarious point, a reticence and an understanding about the ways of the young and the adolescent – which may have engendered a sense of false security – to find that criticism and ridicule and scepticism had merely been sharpened in the years of waiting, years in which the needs of circulation among a newspaper readership which had lost its deference, except to older and trusted members of the royal family, meant the more disclosed, the merrier. Prince Andrew came out into the world self-confidently and apparently equipped for a lot. But he was not equipped for that.

Facing page: The princes, Andrew and Edward climbing trees in the gardens of Buckingham Palace. From a series of photographs taken to mark Prince Andrew's sixth birthday. Every day as a break from lessons in the school-room the young boys were sent out to play in the extensive Palace gardens.

So there have been sold and printed all the stories, true and half true, that a public, open to charm and persuasion and also open to imagination and titillation, has been ready to buy. If half of what biographies, gossip and memoirs have said about more important people in the past had come out in their early twenties, they might not have gone on to be important. What Prince Andrew has faced, and the Princess and he face now together, is the test of living with media that do not like having their preconceptions disturbed, that are distrustful of any such disturbance, and that devoutly hope he and she will go on giving them good copy and will not depart into obscurity and tranquillity.

When Prince Andrew was born at Buckingham Palace on 19 February 1960, he was the first son born to a reigning sovereign since 1857. The baby prince was christened Andrew Albert Christian Edward. He was an energetic and inquisitive child, playing in the Palace garden and uprooting part of it. He was encouraged to ride ponies from an early age but preferred swimming. He played football along the corridors of the Palace. 'Every now and then,' he was to say, 'a pane of glass got broken but I don't think we ever broke a piece of Meissen china.'

Right: Prince Andrew at Smith's Lawn, Windsor Great Park with a young friend. The Queen often brought her young children to watch Prince Philip and Prince Charles play polo and during matches the children amused themselves playing around on the grass among the horseboxes.

Right: The Queen and Prince Andrew watching the games at the Braemar Highland Gathering which takes place not far from Balmoral in September every year. Prince Andrew always looked forward to his annual summer holiday at Balmoral and still has a special affection for the place and its people.

Below: In August 1969 Prince Andrew enjoyed an informal seaside holiday at Bembridge on the Isle of Wight, staying with the family of one of his former school-room companions, Katie Seymour. Prince Andrew played on the beach like any other small child and went for fishing trips in the Solent on the Seymour's boat.

When he was eight he was sent off to Heatherdown preparatory school at Ascot, and found it precisely the life for him, as he did, when, at thirteen, he went on to his father's old public school, Gordonstoun, the school that Prince Charles had so disliked. There, on his second day, he got the nickname that was to stick: 'Randy Andy'. The school had just gone co-educational, and the rule was that boys were not allowed into the girls' house. The prince did not know that, walked in to say hello – and that was that. He has always spoken affectionately of 'the frontier ladies of Gordonstoun, as in the days of the Gold Rush', but thought his nickname quite unfair then and since. While at Gordonstoun, he joined the coastguards, won his wings as an Air Training Corps glider pilot, and was captain of cricket.

Canada was to Prince Andrew what Australia had been to Prince Charles: the place where he found the outside world. This was at Lakefield College, Ontario, also an Outward Bound type of school, where he made enduring friendships with both sexes. He worked on a farm one holiday. Years later he went back, canoeing in the Rockies accompanied by a friend and his old headmaster. Those who knew the Prince found him after Lakefield more thoughtful, more considerate and more responsible. Now his mind was set on joining the Royal Navy.

A family photograph taken by Lord Lichfield at Balmoral in the summer of 1972 to mark the Queen's silver wedding anniversary. Balmoral has been a favourite royal residence since it was bought by Queen Victoria in 1852. Every generation since then, the royal family have 'gone native' during their visits to the castle, wearing kilts, tweeds and tartans.

Prince Andrew in Canada

Left and below left: Described by Prince Charles as 'the one with the Robert Redford looks', Prince Andrew emerged as a new teenage idol during his visit to Canada in 1976, his first overseas tour with his parents. Below right: During their visit to the Olympic Games he was escorted by Sandi Jones with whom the Prince kept in touch on subsequent trips to Canada. Far below: The success of the tour led to Prince Andrew spending two terms at Lakefield College, near Ontario in 1977. He played rugby there among other sports and took to acting, as Mr Brownlow with side whiskers in the musical Oliver.

Facing page above left and right: Staying with a friend, Peter Lorriman and his family, Prince Andrew sampled genuine maple syrup from a sap-collection pail. Centre: After the summer term ended he went on a 300-mile canoe trip down the Coppermine River to the Arctic. Below: He later met up with Prince Charles at the Calgary Stampede where they dressed for the part in stetsons and bootlace ties.

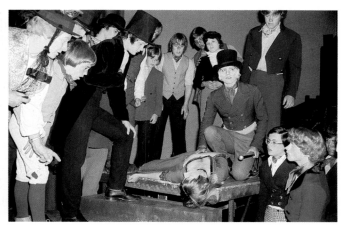

Facing page: An official photograph taken to mark Prince Andrew's eighteenth birthday.

Above and below left: Prince Andrew on his first day at the Royal Naval College, Dartmouth in September 1979 and during his passing-out parade.

Above right: Prince Andrew during his two-week parachute course.

Below right: Prince Philip proudly awarding Prince Andrew his flying wings as a qualified helicopter pilot.

Helicopters had always fascinated him, from his early trips with the Queen's Flight, and the Navy offered a greater variety of helicopter work than the other two services. He reported for aptitude tests in December 1978, and passed with ease. Like so many royal midshipmen before him, he entered the Royal Naval College at Dartmouth, and learned, like them, what it was to be taken down a peg. But Prince Andrew stuck in. He had an acclimatization cruise in the aircraft carrier HMS *Hermes,* a Marine Commando course on Dartmoor, a survival training course, and five months' flying at RAF Leeming, in Yorkshire. He got not only his 'wings' – but the silver salver for the midshipman with the highest marks. Prince Philip proudly did the presentation, telling him: 'This is only the beginning'. It was. Prince Andrew joined HMS *Invincible* and took part in a Nato exercise off the Norwegian coast. One month later, in March 1982, the Falklands crisis began.

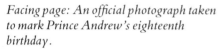

HMS Invincible, *one of the largest ships in the Royal Navy, was Prince Andrew's home on and off for nearly two years, including the six-month-long Falklands Campaign and a goodwill visit to the United States and the Caribbean. The ship's company numbered nearly 1,000 men and Prince Andrew was treated like any other young officer. To his fellow officers on board, he was known simply as 'H', short for His Royal Highness.*

The *Invincible* sailed from Portsmouth with the Task Force en route to the Falklands and Prince Andrew sailed with her. His quarters were on 2 Deck, just below where the Sea Harriers landed. It began as a jaunt while the diplomats tried to contrive a peaceful settlement.

When *Invincible* passed south over the Equator he was ducked along with others who had not crossed the line before. In the Crossing the Line show, his crime was pronounced to be: 'Positioning yourself in front of the cameras so that your mum will see you on the telly'. Then the war began in earnest in the rough seas and the chill of the South Atlantic.

'A full set of whiskers' is permissible in the Navy but Prince Andrew, to his intense annoyance, was ordered to shave his off by his commanding officer.

Prince Andrew's Sea King helicopter winching a Land Rover on board HMS Invincible. *Prince Andrew and his crew, a co-pilot, observer and aircrewman, were one of fourteen flying crews on board whose duties included anti-submarine fighting, fetching and carrying men and supplies, conducting search and rescue missions in the sea and, above all, during the Falklands Campaign acting as decoy targets for the deadly Exocet missiles launched by the Argentinians.*

The first duty of the Prince's Sea King helicopter was to fly on anti-submarine missions. The Argentine navy had effective German-built submarines, and with only the two carriers to give the Task Force any air cover, the commander, Rear-Admiral Sandy Woodward, needed to keep them off at all costs or the expedition would end in disaster. There were reports of Argentine activity but it came to nothing, except in regular Argentine claims that each of the carriers had been sunk. In this propaganda war the fact that the Prince was serving in the *Invincible* was of primary importance. In London, the Pope, visiting the Queen at

Prince Andrew at the controls of his Sea King helicopter. On board HMS Invincible *Prince Andrew was the youngest officer in 820 Squadron and comparatively inexperienced but, according to his commanding officer, he was 'an above-average pilot, professional and very sound'.*

Sublieutenant HRH The Prince Andrew with fellow officers of 820 Squadron on board HMS Invincible *on her triumphant return to England in September 1982 after cessation of hostilities in the South Atlantic.*

Buckingham Palace, told her he prayed for her son's safety. Whatever their own wishes, princes are not often risked under enemy fire, although his grandfather, the future George VI, had directed a gun turret in the battleship *Collingwood* at Jutland in 1916. Prince Andrew accepted his risks off the Falklands like everyone else.

The weather was appalling. Two Sea Harriers took off and were lost. When the Argentine air force came out the call for Action Stations became ever more frequent. The Prince said afterwards: 'To be told to lie down on the deck of a ship is the most lonely feeling I know, waiting for the bang or the all clear'. He was in the air when the destroyer *Sheffield* was hit amidships by an Exocet missile, and watched, appalled, as the smoke rose from her: 'For the first ten minutes after *Sheffield* was hit, we really didn't know which way to turn or what to do. I was fairly frightened. It was a dreadful sight. It's something I thought I would never see, a British warship devastated'.

The Royal party coming ashore from HMS Invincible. *A patriotic Croydon florist presented all the ship's company with a red rose as they came ashore and the Queen and Princess Anne were presented with baskets of matching roses.*

The drill for keeping the Exocets away from the carriers was to put the helicopters in the air to act as decoys. The missiles would turn on them as the nearest target, whereupon the helicopter under attack would lift above the missile and let it go harmlessly underneath on its misdirected way. That was the idea. It was an exercise that needed the coolest judgment. Three times the Task Force's defensive Sea Wolf missiles locked on to the Prince's helicopter when on decoy duty. That was not part of the plan. He said later: 'It's not much fun having one of those fellows pick you out as a target. It really makes the hair stand up on the back of your neck'.

When, instead of the *Invincible*, it was the support ship *Atlantic Conveyor* that the Argentines managed to sink, his helicopter rescued twenty-six men from the sea. 'It was something,' he said, 'I shall never, ever forget. It was horrific. I saw my ship, *Invincible,* firing her missiles. It was my most frightening moment of the war'. For the seamen they picked up, some burned, some injured, all dazed, it was quite a moment to see just who the helicopter's co-pilot was.

The spontaneous reaction of a jubilant prince as he came ashore. With Royal Marine bands playing on the dockside and cheering crowds greeting the royal party and returning heroes it was a patriotic and highly emotional scene.

Above left: Led by the Queen, Prince Andrew and other members of the royal family attended a service at St Paul's Cathedral in June 1985 to dedicate a memorial to those who had died during the Falklands Conflict three years earlier. As a Falklands Campaign veteran, Prince Andrew laid a wreath during the service on behalf of the Falkland Islanders.

Above right: In 1983 Prince Andrew joined the frigate HMS Brazen as the pilot of the only helicopter on board, a small two-man Lynx. The helicopter was affectionately known on board as the 'Brazen Hussy'.

When the Argentine forces surrendered, Prince Andrew took the chance to see Port Stanley, the islands' small capital, and said jokingly: 'It's the perfect place to bring my bride on honeymoon'. He telephoned the Queen at Buckingham Palace and spoke to her for a quarter-of-an-hour. And later the Queen, Prince Philip and Princess Anne were all at Portsmouth when the *Invincible*, towering above the narrow harbour entrance, came triumphantly home. Every man who came ashore was presented with a red rose. The Prince carried his in his teeth, as did all those with kit to carry. It was time for leave, and home, and friends – and the memory of what it had meant: 'During those moments when there was fear I overcame it with the simple maxim that I must think positive. I told myself I'm going to survive this'.

In January 1985 he went back to the Falklands as a Lynx helicopter pilot (and entertainments officer) in the frigate HMS *Brazen,* operating in the exclusion zone. It was normal duty for a professional naval officer who had signed up for a twelve-year stint. On one flight a hydraulic pump failed and he had to land in a remote field in East Falkland. The Defence Ministry later said: 'This is what we would expect of an officer of his experience and seniority'.

But Prince Andrew was a little more senior than that. When the time came to open the new £400-million airport at Mount Pleasant to take wide-bodied, troop-carrying jets, he was the local member of the royal family required to do the job. It was quite a turn: he compared the airport with the pioneering days of the American West and, drawing on experience, said it was the next most difficult place in the world after St Helena to build one. After the airport, Prince Andrew laid a wreath at the cemetery at San Carlos, paid visits to the islands' first commercial woollen mill at Fox Bay and to a new school hostel at Port Stanley, and unveiled a plaque inaugurating the new hospital, costing £6.5 million, to replace the old King Edward hospital that had been destroyed by fire. Then it was promptly back to normal service.

With HMS Brazen *Prince Andrew returned to the Falkland Islands for a second, peacetime tour of duty. Before returning to England in May 1985 he undertook several public engagements, including attending the Blue Beach Memorial Ceremony.*

Prince Andrew left the *Brazen* and his helicopter, nicknamed the 'Brazen Hussy', in March 1986 to join a course at the Royal Naval College, Greenwich; and, of course, to plan for the great day. The *Brazen*'s crew gave him a surprising send-off – apparently a surprise to him, though not to the television cameras waiting for him – complete with a number, sung to the tune of 'I'm the King of the Swingers':

> I am the Prince of the Hussy-oh,
> An airborne VIP.
> I am over the top – have had to stop;
> And that's what's bothering me.

It was an affectionate parting on both sides. His shipmates had always known him as 'H', being short for HRH, and he had even got Selina Scott, the well-known television presenter to put kisses on a helicopter section for them. Prince Andrew intends to stay in the Navy for the time being and his wife has encouraged him to do so. But it cannot be quite the same again.

Prince Andrew being given a surprise send-off from HMS Brazen, *a singing and dancing revue on the flightdeck. Only days before the announcement of his engagement he was leaving the ship after two years to attend a short lieutenant's course at the Royal Naval College, Greenwich.*

Life in the Navy sparked off Prince Andrew's current enthusiasm for photography. He is seen here in Port Stanley on the Falkland Islands during his second tour of duty there in 1984. Such was his enthusiasm for his new hobby that he was rarely seen on board without a camera except when flying his helicopter or on official duties.

Below left: Prince Andrew seen leaving Mr Gene Nocon's photographic studio in London, clutching a portfolio of his photographs. Mr Nocon, a professional photographer has given Prince Andrew much advice and encouragement and the Prince has spent many hours in his basement darkroom, perfecting his hobby.

Below right: Prince Andrew at the launch party for his book, Photographs *in September 1985. Described by him as 'a small slice of autobiography, recording memories and impressions', the book includes many informal family photographs and some taken during his travels in the United States and Canada.*

It was the Falklands war that first turned Prince Andrew's thoughts to photography (he did not have a camera with him at the time); that, and his friend, Miss Koo Stark. He bought his first camera in 1983, set up a darkroom (really his bathroom) at Buckingham Palace and tried his hand, privately, for three or four months where he knew he could not be seen. That is why the first section of his book in aid of charity, *Photographs,* is called 'Windows, Roofs and Gardens'. But he soon launched out on wider topics starting on his Canadian canoeing trip.

The Prince prefers to take black and white photographs, and has done some unusual ones of his family, although he insists he does not like to pester them because they get enough of photographers every day anyway. In return, he has had his family's patronage – not an unmixed advantage for a young man still having to learn from his mistakes.

The critics were carping when he took the official photographs for the first birthday of his godson and nephew, Prince Harry, in September 1985. The pictures were taken on the deck of the royal yacht *Britannia* while the royal family were on their summer cruise round the Western Isles of Scotland – which might account for certain of the shortcomings. Faults were swiftly found on every side. The young Prince's eyes were too dark; his toes had been cut off; the rope of his swing covered his ear. Anyway, the critics said, they were all out of focus. The Prince's view: 'I think it is a natural photograph of a small one-year-old boy'. But he persevered. His mother, the Queen, stood up for him and told him to take the pictures for her sixtieth birthday. She liked them.

Above: The young photographer at the Royal Windsor Horse Show in 1973. The Queen is an enthusiastic amateur photographer herself, and ten years later, gave Prince Andrew much support when he began to take his new hobby seriously. She even gave him her priceless Hasselblad camera which he succeeded in damaging when he started to play around with its mechanism.

Such was the Queen's delight in Prince Andrew's developing talent that she commissioned her son to take the official photographs to commemorate her sixtieth birthday in April 1986. The photograph was taken during the family's New Year holiday at Sandringham.

The laughing Prince

Traditionally the royal family have always been keen on practical jokes and Prince Andrew is no exception. Left: Being presented with a stetson during a visit to the MGM studios in Los Angeles. Below left: Guests also come in for the Prince's particular brand of humour. This time Prince Andrew had put a flower down the bodice of Mrs Margaret Trudeau, the wife of the Canadian prime minister. Below right: Prince Andrew enjoying a joke with his sister. He has always had a close relationship with Princess Anne, despite the ten-year gap in age.

Facing page above left: When he attended the trials for the America's Cup in 1983 Prince Andrew was surrounded by a bevy of beautiful girls, all hoping to become his next girlfriend. Above right: Prince Charles poking fun at Prince Andrew, aided by his polo stick. Centre left: Laughing with the actors, Michael York and Roger Moore. Centre right: Even greeting a prize-winning Jersey cow called Sybil caused Prince Andrew amusement during his 1985 tour of New Brunswick in Canada. Below: Sharing a joke with his fiancée at the Royal Windsor Horse Trials in May. Miss Ferguson's stepmother said at the time of the engagement, 'I'm sure that one ingredient of their marriage is that they will have a lot of fun together'.

The Queen even gave him her Hasselblad camera, which he did not improve by tinkering with its mechanism. The Prince has five Nikons of his own, so it came as no surprise when the Japanese asked him to open their new plant at Kingston upon Thames, Surrey. He gave the professionals a good royal reaction shot when the firm presented him with a gold-plated product of theirs, priced at a simple £2,500. He decided to keep the camera, the Palace officials said afterwards, as a 'token gift'.

Aspiring photographers need to have models, and some find good-looking young female models a particular challenge to their skill. And young women, usually described as of the 'vivacious' sort, who are models tend to need publicity. And there are always newspapers ready to oblige them. This makes for a tangled web which Prince Andrew either did not understand at the beginning or blithely thought he could ignore. There is no doubt he found Miss Stark a very agreeable friend and she, in turn, helped him develop his photography by putting him in touch with Mr Gene Nocon, the expert from California, at his London studio. It was also great fun, in compiling his portfolio, to get Miss Finola Hughes to play an alluring ghost in the Windsor Castle dungeons, and to persuade Miss Kate Rabett, now Mrs Hesketh-Harvey, to dress up in a blonde wig and a wet suit in the lake at Frogmore, as if she were accepting the return of Excalibur. These and other tasteful scenes, which the good Pre-Raphaelites might have understood and even appreciated, duly appeared in *Photographs*. The difficulty was that other pictures of the young women, and accompanying text, had already appeared in the papers. It is often hard to distinguish between life and art.

The actress, Miss Koo Stark was a regular girlfriend of Prince Andrew for several years. She is a keen photographer herself and encouraged Prince Andrew to develop his hobby, introducing him to Mr Nocon. She has remained loyal to the Prince ever since by maintaining a discreet silence about their long friendship.

Above left: The actress, Miss Kate Rabett at the launch party for the Ilford calendar which Prince Andrew was commissioned to do in 1985. The calendar included a series of photographs of top models and actresses. In one photograph Miss Rabett posed as the Lady of the Lake, accepting the return of Excalibur by standing in the lake at Frogmore, wearing a fantastic wig and wet suit.

Above right: The six-foot tall Prince, called the world's most eligible bachelor after Prince Charles's marriage in 1981, has been linked by the press with attractive young ladies wherever he has gone. One lady was the model, Clare Park who was chosen by Prince Andrew for the month of July in his Ilford Calendar.

It is something that has been seen to. Miss Stark, loyally keeping her mouth shut, has disappeared from the scene (except for the least imaginative of news editors), married and then, unhappily, unmarried. Others like Miss Vicki Hodge, the most vivacious of them all, have taken their money from their employers and departed. The Prince has said, 'If I take a girl out to dinner newspapers tend to jump to conclusions rather quicker than they should'. It may be he would have to say that, but he knows he need not expect them to change their ways.

The positive side of the Prince's photography is that he has become a property. His name does not hinder things. He took the pictures of the combined twenty-first birthday party of Lady Sarah Armstrong-Jones, Lady Helen Windsor, Prince Edward and Mr James Ogilvy, all in the close family, at Windsor Castle. His work has been exhibited at the Hamiltons and Barbican galleries. He was commissioned to do the smart Ilford calendar one year. He earned £1,100 from *Life* magazine for his photographs. He is not a rival to Lord Snowdon (who has also been helpful) yet, but give him time. Naturally, the old school would much prefer he kept to studies of the Queen and her dogs out on a windy day beside his helicopter at Balmoral. That's what's called acceptable. They might not quite go along, though, with his explanation: 'The Balmoral photograph was taken when I was on my way back to my ship in Glasgow, and we stopped for a cup of tea – and, more importantly, to go to the loo.' Quite. It was a young man speaking, but an honest one.

The Royal Family
showing HRH Prince Andrew's descent from King James I

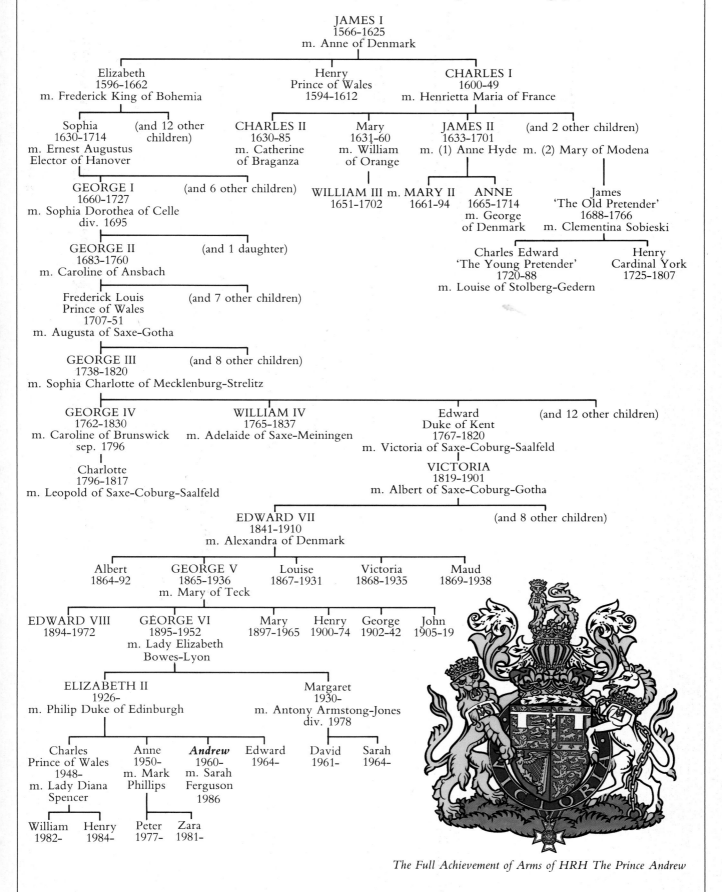

JAMES I
1566-1625
m. Anne of Denmark

Elizabeth
1596-1662
m. Frederick King of Bohemia

Henry
Prince of Wales
1594-1612

CHARLES I
1600-49
m. Henrietta Maria of France

Sophia
1630-1714
m. Ernest Augustus
Elector of Hanover

(and 12 other children)

CHARLES II
1630-85
m. Catherine
of Braganza

Mary
1631-60
m. William
of Orange

JAMES II
1633-1701
m. (1) Anne Hyde m. (2) Mary of Modena

(and 2 other children)

GEORGE I
1660-1727
m. Sophia Dorothea of Celle
div. 1695

(and 6 other children)

WILLIAM III m. MARY II
1651-1702   1661-94

ANNE
1665-1714
m. George
of Denmark

James
'The Old Pretender'
1688-1766
m. Clementina Sobieski

GEORGE II
1683-1760
m. Caroline of Ansbach

(and 1 daughter)

Charles Edward
'The Young Pretender'
1720-88
m. Louise of Stolberg-Gedern

Henry
Cardinal York
1725-1807

Frederick Louis
Prince of Wales
1707-51
m. Augusta of Saxe-Gotha

(and 7 other children)

GEORGE III
1738-1820
m. Sophia Charlotte of Mecklenburg-Strelitz

(and 8 other children)

GEORGE IV
1762-1830
m. Caroline of Brunswick
sep. 1796

WILLIAM IV
1765-1837
m. Adelaide of Saxe-Meiningen

Edward
Duke of Kent
1767-1820
m. Victoria of Saxe-Coburg-Saalfeld

(and 12 other children)

Charlotte
1796-1817
m. Leopold of Saxe-Coburg-Saalfeld

VICTORIA
1819-1901
m. Albert of Saxe-Coburg-Gotha

EDWARD VII
1841-1910
m. Alexandra of Denmark

(and 8 other children)

Albert
1864-92

GEORGE V
1865-1936
m. Mary of Teck

Louise
1867-1931

Victoria
1868-1935

Maud
1869-1938

EDWARD VIII
1894-1972

GEORGE VI
1895-1952
m. Lady Elizabeth
Bowes-Lyon

Mary
1897-1965

Henry
1900-74

George
1902-42

John
1905-19

ELIZABETH II
1926-
m. Philip Duke of Edinburgh

Margaret
1930-
m. Antony Armstong-Jones
div. 1978

Charles
Prince of Wales
1948-
m. Lady Diana
Spencer

Anne
1950-
m. Mark
Phillips

Andrew
1960-
m. Sarah
Ferguson
1986

Edward
1964-

David
1961-

Sarah
1964-

William
1982-

Henry
1984-

Peter
1977-

Zara
1981-

The Full Achievement of Arms of HRH The Prince Andrew

THE BRIDE

PEOPLE like her. It is her greatest asset. It is what will make her a success in her royal career. Her red hair and blue eyes mean she will never go unremarked. But the public's perception of her in the brief months since she became public property is that she is fun; not an intellectual certainly, not bookish or shy or stuck-up either, but fun – and very much her own woman. She smiles generously and often, as if she likes the people she is smiling at. Dressing-up is not an obsession; she seems most at home with the simple and the casual. She seems the sort that prefers to spend wet afternoons outside.

As princesses necessarily come in all shapes and sizes, there is much that is reassuring about the new Princess Andrew, including her shape. There is that something about her which indicates that she knows how to enjoy herself, and knows also just how to cope with the rather formidable young man who is her husband. She has manners too. Through all the weeks of being pursued by the press and the photographers before her engagement she was not heard to say a wrong word, whatever she might be thinking. What would have made anyone wilt brought out the best in her. It was not a great surprise when she told a friend: 'I'm loving every minute of it.' That self-confidence was not misplaced. Sarah Ferguson came through with flying colours, and the public saw in her just what it wanted: a new princess who was quite a character.

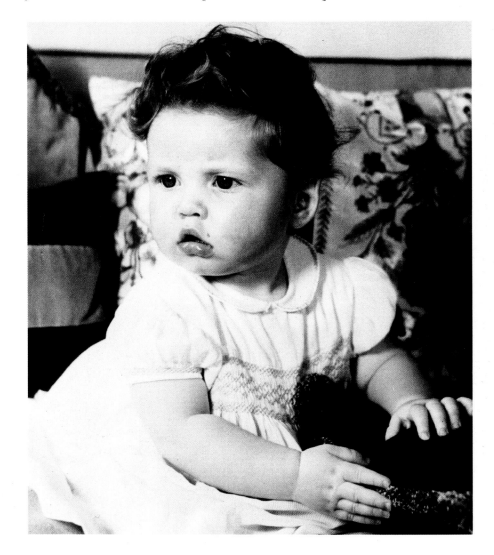

Her twenty-six years have been spent conventionally; conventional, that is, for her set. But they have shown her to be independent when it mattered to her. That is appealing, especially to those of her own age. What the Prince's great-grandmother, the formidable Queen Mary, would have thought of some of her independence is another matter. What counts is that the Prince's mother has accepted her for what she is, and seems to have thought she would be good for her son, and to have thought so for some time before her son did.

Sarah Margaret Ferguson was born in London on 15 October 1959, the second daughter of an army family, and a courtier family. Her father,

On page 42: Miss Ferguson in the White Drawing-room at Buckingham Palace. She is proudly displaying her diamond and ruby engagement ring chosen to complement her flowing, red hair.

On page 43: A charming photograph of Sarah Ferguson taken shortly after her first birthday. She was born at the private Welbeck Clinic in London's Marylebone on 15 October 1959 and several days later, returned with her mother to their home at Lowood, Sunningdale, near Ascot. Her father, Ronald Ferguson, then a captain in The Life Guards, did not register his second daughter's birth until six weeks later.

Left: 'Daddy's little girl' – Sarah, aged ten months, sitting on her father's lap on the banks of the river Thames.

Dummer Down Farm, the Ferguson family home near Basingstoke in Hampshire. Sarah's father inherited the elegant Georgian farmhouse and 800-acre farm on the death of her grandfather, Colonel Andrew Ferguson in 1966. The comfortable farmhouse is situated just in front of the farm buildings and looks over green, rolling countryside. Sarah's grandmother, Lady Elmhirst also lives in the beautiful village of Dummer.

Major Ronald Ferguson, followed three previous generations into the Life Guards, and ended by commanding the Sovereign's Escort. Her mother, now Mrs Susan Barrantes, was a cavalry officer's daughter. The family was never less than comfortably off, though not, it seems, ostentatiously so. When his father died in 1966 Major Ferguson inherited the 1,200-acre estate at Dummer Down Farm, in Hampshire (just south-west of Basingstoke on the M3), and chose to end his twenty years with the Life Guards to manage the estate. But leaving the army did not mean giving up his connection with the royal family. Major Ferguson now runs the Guards Polo Club at Smith's Lawn, Windsor. He is also Prince Charles's polo manager, and may have hoped to manage his household. He is friendly with Prince Philip. He has been, above all, a man the royal family know and trust, and can identify his qualities in his daughter.

Prince Charles with Major Ronald Ferguson, his polo manager for the past ten years. Major Ferguson became a close friend of Prince Philip when he was a young polo player of great ability in the 1950s. He now runs the Guards Polo Club at Smith's Lawn, one of England's premier polo clubs.

The Ferguson Family Album

Behind Miss Ferguson's ready smile and well-developed sense of humour lies a solid family history. *Right:* Her grandfather, Colonel Andrew Ferguson on his wedding day to Miss Marian Scott, the granddaughter of the 6th Duke of Buccleuch. Later he commanded the Sovereign's Escort of The Life Guards, as did his son, Major Ronald Ferguson later on, and served with distinction in the Second World War. *Below left:* Young Ronald Ferguson aged three years. It is interesting to see the resemblance between Sarah and her father at the same age. *Below right:* Young Ronald on the beach with his mother in July 1933.

Facing page above left: A portrait of Ronald Ferguson and his brother, John, dressed as pages for a family wedding. *Above right:* Ronald Ferguson's Aunt Jane who later married William Fellowes, the Queen's previous land agent at Sandringham. Their son, Robert is married to Lady Jane Spencer, the sister of the Princess of Wales. *Below:* Young Ronald and his brother John.

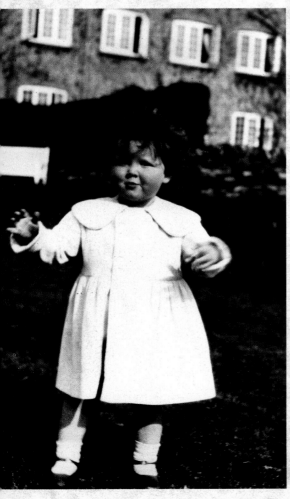

Right: Sarah's great-grandfather, General Algernon Ferguson with his two grandchildren, Ronald and John and Spider, the dog. Below left: A portrait of young Ronald Ferguson painted in 1943. It now hangs on the wall at Dummer Down Farm. Below right: Sarah's mother, Susan Wright aged six weeks old. The Wright family can be traced back as far as 1559.

Facing page above left and right: Molly Bishop, a cousin of Ronald Ferguson's mother, was commissioned to do these portraits of Sarah's parents on their engagement in 1955. Both pictures hang on the wall at Dummer Down Farm. Below left: The marriage of Major Ronald Ferguson and Miss Susan Wright took place at St Margaret's, Westminster in 1956. The elegant bride was just eighteen years old. Below right: The front cover of The Tatler in January 1957 showed Sarah's mother, the newly married Mrs Ronald Ferguson.

The TATLER & BYSTANDER

JAN. 16, 1957
TWO SHILLINGS

MRS RONALD FERGUSON

Nanny remembers . . .

While by no means rich, the Ferguson family were certainly well-to-do, employing a cook, gardener and a Finnish nanny, Ritva Risu who came over to England when she was twenty-two years old. Left: Jane and Sarah (on the right) photographed with Miss Risu who remembers: 'My first impression of the children was that they were so well behaved. They never caused the slightest trouble. Sarah was always my favourite, she was just so good and gentle, even as a little girl.' Below: Major and Mrs Ronald Ferguson with their two girls on the doorstep of Lowood House, Sunningdale. Photographed by Miss Risu who bought her first camera while working for the Fergusons. She could not quite master the art of centring her subject matter!
Facing page above: Sarah, Jane and their cousin (in the middle) with Miss Risu and a friend enjoying a day out at Stonehenge.
Facing page below: Young Sarah brushing her hair at her mother's dressing-table at Lowood. Miss Risu called her 'My little Redhair' and even as a toddler, she had the fiery nature of a redhead.

These photographs were all taken by Miss Risu while she was looking after the Ferguson girls. Facing page above left: Almost as soon as they could walk Jane and Sarah were taught to ride on their pony. Above right: Sarah on a pony while visiting relations near Salisbury, Wiltshire. Below left: Even the rocking horse was ridden with enthusiasm. Below right: Sarah sitting next to Miss Morton (Mortie), the cook at Lowood. The dog, Puff sits on her lap. Mortie was very much part of the family and everybody was very fond of her.

Above left: Jane and Sarah with the puppies, Puff and Carrie. Above right: Mrs Ferguson with Puff and Carrie at Lowood. Centre left: The two girls painting with watercolours outside on a sunny day. Centre right: Playing with their teddy bears. Below: Playing in the park near Lowood. While the two girls played well together, Miss Risu noticed that Sarah tended to dominate her elder sister. 'Sarah usually got her own way,' says Miss Risu. 'She was much more lively than Jane. She was full of energy and had a great sense of humour. Jane was more ladylike while Sarah was something of a tomboy.'

Sarah, aged ten, with her first pony. Both her parents were excellent riders and encouraged the two girls to learn from an early age.

It so happens that Prince Andrew, like Prince Charles, has married a childhood acquaintance. It makes sense. Now that the days of arranged marriages with foreign royal stock are long gone, it helps to have a basis of shared memories, and of shared family friendship; it certainly helps in getting parental and grandparental approval. Prince Andrew and Miss Ferguson were of an age together at Smith's Lawn on the long summer afternoons when their fathers were playing polo, even if they may not have had much else in common. So her mother was entirely right when, presaging the engagement announcement, she said they had met at polo, adding: 'Doesn't everyone?' Her daughter, naturally, learned to ride at gymkhanas, pony clubs and junior trials. She was good at it. Her father has recalled how 'she used to go absolutely straight and take crashing falls, and would sit on the ground beating it with frustration.' She could tell when it was her fault she had fallen off. That candour seems to have remained.

Sarah and her mother taking part in a pairs event. Her mother says proudly that Sarah is one of the most natural riders you could ever hope to find, and the school holidays at Dummer were filled with many hours of riding and taking part in local gymkhanas.

Sarah as a young competitor. She even represented her preparatory school in the All-England Schools Championship at Hickstead one year.

Her school days were unexceptionable, and nothing that her headmistresses or school friends have recalled publicly from those years makes her out to have been other than one of her set. She went first to Daneshill, a mixed preparatory school at Basingstoke, Hampshire where her small stepbrother and sister now go, twenty years on. She was good at most sports, but excelled at riding, representing the school at the All-England Schools Championship at Hickstead. She went on to Hurst Lodge, a small, red-brick boarding school near Ascot. The school had a reputation for art and drama, and so attracted the daughters of entertainers. She had an aptitude for drawing, took ballet lessons, but seems to have preferred modern dancing.

She was no slouch in class, taking six O-levels in Art, English Language, English Literature, Spoken English, French and Biology. Not all were in the most testing of subjects, but her examination attainment puts her at no disadvantage in the royal family. She rose to be joint head girl in 1976 (voted on by both staff and pupils) and netball captain. When her father congratulated her on being head girl, saying it must be because she was a responsible sort, she had her answer: 'No, I was so uncontrollable they had to make me head girl, so I would start behaving.'

Above: Sarah's mother with her husband, Señor Hector Barrantes, the Argentine international polo player. When Sarah was fourteen, her mother announced that she had fallen in love with Señor Barrantes and would be moving to live in Buenos Aires. The couple now divide their time between Buenos Aires and a remote 1,000-acre ranch where they breed horses and raise crops.

It was when she was thirteen and starting her second year at Hurst Lodge that her mother decided to end the marriage (after eighteen years) and marry her Argentine international polo player, Señor Barrantes. Broken marriages were not unusual in that circle, and this one was conducted in a civilized way for the daughters' sake, but it was a test. Her father's recollection of the time does her credit: 'Neither of them were difficult children and I think the crisis had more effect on Jane than Sarah . . . Sarah didn't openly react to her mother's departure, and I don't think it changed the way she was, but of course she was affected by it.'

The divorce resulted in her seeing a lot of her father and sharing his interests, which meant seeing a lot of Smith's Lawn and its polo set. Her sister, Jane married an Australian polo player, Mr Alex Makim. Major Ferguson remarried in 1976 and Sarah found her stepmother to be a friend. Mrs Susan Ferguson is grateful to her: 'It says much for Fergie's big heart that she welcomed me as her stepmother with great enthusiasm, even though she was very close to her real mother.' The Prince of Wales is now godfather to Mrs Ferguson's youngest daughter, Eliza; both he and the Princess of Wales were at the christening in February. The royal family is nothing if not an extended family.

Sarah, aged sixteen, as chief bridesmaid at her sister's wedding to the Australian polo player, Mr Alex Makim. After her wedding, Jane moved to live on her husband's remote family farm in northern New South Wales. She now has two children, the elder of whom, Seamus was chosen to be a page boy at the royal wedding.

After school it was a matter, as for most girls of her crowd, of training to earn a living before making a suitable marriage. Her aims were modest. She started at a secretarial college in London, trying her hand at typing, shorthand and book-keeping. Proficiency was slow in coming. She and her friend Miss Charlotte Eden (now Mrs Mungo McGowan), daughter of the Conservative junior minister, Sir John Eden, sat at the back of the class and duly found themselves at the bottom of the class. The school's confidential assessment of her may even have got her right: 'Bright, bouncy redhead. She's a bit slapdash. But has initiative and personality which she will well use to her advantage when she gets older. Accepts responsibility happily.' But she was a slow starter. A cookery course seems to have brought no advantageous entry into the wage-earning classes.

She and Miss Eden set off to Argentina to visit her mother and her husband in their home near Buenos Aires, where they farm and breed horses. She gets on well with her stepfather, and her mother is naturally proud of her: 'We don't see each other as often as we would like, but the mother-daughter bond is very tight indeed.' After that first visit she and Miss Eden set off by bus to Rio de Janeiro, along bumpy country roads,

Above: Sarah photographed while staying with her mother and stepfather in Argentina before setting off with her friend, Charlotte McGowan on an adventurous, four-month bus journey from Buenos Aires to Rio de Janeiro in Brazil.

Major and Mrs Ronald Ferguson on their wedding day in 1976. Sarah welcomed her stepmother, Susan Deptford, the daughter of a Norfolk farmer, with great enthusiasm even though she was close to her real mother. They are now the greatest of friends. Mrs Ferguson said, 'Sarah made me welcome from the start.'

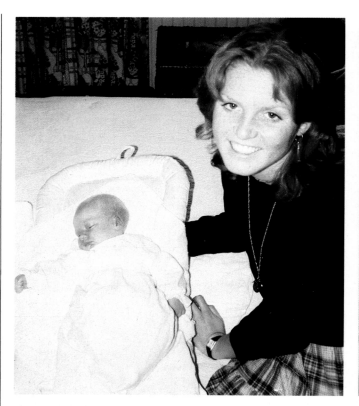

Above left: A photograph of Sarah in her early twenties, taken after a holiday abroad. The photograph sits in a silver frame on a side table in the drawing-room at Dummer Down Farm.

Above right: Mr Kim Smith-Bingham photographed in 1978. Sarah first met this courteous and cultivated Old Etonian in Argentina during her visit to her mother in 1977. Three years later he became her first boyfriend, sending her red roses and Valentine cards.

Facing page: Sarah delighted in her new extended family. She is seen here (above left) with her young half-brother Andrew in October 1978 and (above right) with her stepmother, Susan and half-brother Andrew in the garden at Dummer Down Farm. Below: A family gathering at Dummer, Christmas 1983.

with peasants and their smaller livestock for company, taking weeks on the way. Their generation likes to have a great adventure somewhere. This was hers. After that, a penurious stay in the United States before flying home to start the search for a steady job.

She had a time as a 'temp' with a flat-letting agency in south-west London. She was also taken on by a public relations agency in Knightsbridge owned by Mr Neil Durden-Smith, husband of the broadcaster Miss Judith Chalmers (and himself a polo commentator). Her boss there, Mr Peter Cunard, remembers her with a mixture of affection and resignation: 'She incurred my wrath by spending a great deal of time on the phone dealing with her social life, fixing up dinners and nights out.' That, of course, is not unusual among young office girls. But she seems to have worked hard enough, and got promotion. Mr Cunard's verdict is: 'She was totally reliable, thrived on responsibility, and was totally professional.'

It appeared, though, that her social life was still coming first. She chose to take short-term jobs as a secretary-cum-personal assistant, first at a Kensington video company and then at a Covent Garden art gallery. She liked sociable lunches, dinner with friends and dancing afterwards; Annabel's was a favourite club then. She had also taken up skiing with vim and verve, renting a chalet in Verbier, a fashionable Swiss resort, with Miss Laura Smith-Bingham. She had met her brother, Mr Kim Smith-Bingham, in Argentina three years before; now he was in Verbier, too, selling modish sportswear to the upper-class and well-off. He admired her dash and skill on the slopes, and their friendship continued in London. It seems to have been quite a staid romance. He remembers her liking for the theatre (especially *Barnum*) and for films with plenty of dancing in them, such as *Fame*, *Grease* and *Saturday Night Fever*.

Above left: Sarah with her companion for two and a half years, Mr Paddy McNally on board a private yacht in Cannes harbour during the weekend of the Monaco Grand Prix, April 1985. Mr McNally, a former racing manager, lives in Switzerland and Sarah often acted as hostess for him at his many famous parties. She was also a wonderful and caring friend to his two teenage sons.

Above right: Sarah on her way to work in the West End of London. Sarah's stepmother has said of her, 'Like her father, Sarah is a great organizer'; and her job, working for the Swiss printing company, BCK as their London directrice, *demanded excellent social contacts, common sense, drive, initiative and a keen commercial eye, all of which she had.*

It was in Verbier, too, that she met Mr Paddy McNally, twenty-two years older than her and a widower with two children, who managed the grand prix champion Niki Lauda and who is still a motor racing consultant. They were regular companions for three years, and she was often the hostess at his parties. Their relationship ended in 1985, and both have been understandably reticent about it. He speaks nothing but good of her: 'She is a girl in a million: level-headed and highly intelligent.' He helped her to get a new job, one she has particularly enjoyed, with BCK, a printing and publishing company based in Geneva, owned by a friend of his, Mr Richard Burton, a former racing driver. She became *directrice* (as her business card says) of BCK's small London office. Before her engagement it was, in fact, a fourth-floor attic office next door to Sothebys, furnished with little more than an answer-phone, a kettle and a cartoon of the Prince and Princess of Wales.

Her job included archive and picture research, liaising with authors and photographers on fine arts books, and securing printing contracts. She is said to have shown she has initiative, drive and a sound commercial eye, as well as excellent social contacts. Mr Burton has been delighted with her: 'Fergie is wonderful at handling people. She is a great asset to the company.' It often meant working all hours, commuting between Geneva and London, and even a visit to the west of the United States on company business last year. Her first thought, on her engage-

As well as being fourth cousins and connected through marriage, the Princess of Wales and Sarah have been close friends for many years. Their friendship developed during long summer afternoons spent watching polo together; during the Princess's courtship by Prince Charles Sarah offered her much comfort and sensible advice on how to cope with the harassment by the press.

ment, was to say she would like to keep the job on if she could. That is a sign of her sensible wish for some independence; whether it is at all practical remains to be seen.

Over these years she stayed in close touch with her father, family and friends, and that meant more afternoons watching polo at Smith's Lawn or Cowdray Park. There she met and talked to, and found she enjoyed talking to, the young Lady Diana Spencer, a new face in that circle and getting to be very much in the news. It emerged that they had a lot in common, in background (even being related by marriage) and upbringing, and, more important, in values and views too. They began to see each other regularly for lunch.

They are probably sufficiently different in experience and looks not to have any sense of rivalry. And they made immediate common cause in the delicate and lengthy business of getting Lady Diana through the nervous months of private courtship and dazzling public engagement until the wedding day. She was considered for the post of being one of the Princess of Wales's ladies-in-waiting, as the Princess seems to have wanted, but, at twenty-one, she was thought to be on the young side. What mattered more was that the friendship continued and deepened after the marriage. She was a regular visitor to Kensington Palace, and was the only guest at the Princess's twenty-first birthday lunch at Buckingham Palace who was not a member of the royal family.

Above left: Mrs Harry Cotterell who as Miss Carolyn Beckwith-Smith was Sarah's flatmate for four years until her engagement to Prince Andrew. During this period the two girls, although outwardly very different, forged a strong and affectionate friendship. Mrs Cotterell was an invaluable ally in helping Sarah evade the press when the speculation mounted after the New Year.

Above right: The sitting-room in the shared flat was a model of good taste and the product of rummaging around junk shops for bargains. Mrs Cotterell furnished the room with a collection of papier-mâché boxes, watercolours of country scenes and vases of fresh flowers to give the room a feeling of airy elegance.

She had also, as the child of a courtier, been drawn closer into the society of courtiers. Needing to find a new, relatively inexpensive home in London, she was recommended by a friend to try Miss Carolyn Beckwith-Smith, a cousin of the Princess's very capable lady-in-waiting, Miss Anne Beckwith-Smith. The house with a spare bedroom turned out to be a flat in Lavender Gardens in upwardly-mobile Clapham in South London, quite near the Junction. It was said they did not seem to have too much else in common at first, apart from a propensity to be late for work. Miss Beckwith-Smith (now Mrs Harry Cotterell) is a vegetarian and an excellent cook; her tenant then was neither. But they got on well. Mrs Cotterell says: 'In all the time I have known her there has never been a cross word. We always said what was on our minds . . . I loved her sense of humour and her feminine intuition.' Her knowledge of the ropes was of particular help when the eyes of the world began to fall on the latest young woman in whom Prince Andrew was understood to be taking a special interest.

If the girls had a dinner party, Sarah did the organization while her flatmate did the cooking. Sarah's taste in food is simple and she prefers it with no frills. For breakfast she likes nothing better than to tuck into a plate of bacon and eggs.

The crowds at Royal Ascot in June 1985.
The Royal Meeting is always a chance for
the royal family to mingle with the guests
in the Royal Enclosure. At the Princess of
Wales's suggestion, the Queen asked
Sarah to join her informal houseparty at
Windsor Castle for Ascot Week in order to
partner Prince Andrew who was home on
leave.

It seemed, of course, to be Prince Andrew's family that was taking most of the interest at the start. Both the Queen and the Princess of Wales wanted her at Windsor for Royal Ascot, in June 1985. She duly appeared at the Royal Meeting, advised by her father to be just herself, and was duly escorted by the Prince on 20 June. He turned out in top hat, morning suit and buttonhole, as required, but without a badge. This was reasonable, since those in the royal carriage procession are not bothered by gatemen or turnstiles, but when Prince Andrew and Miss Ferguson walked from the paddock to the royal enclosure they were stopped, if only briefly: he was, apparently, unrecognized out of naval uniform, and she was just unknown. They were not going to stay like that for much longer.

There is a view held that, for young women eligible for marriage into the royal family, the badgering of the media from the moment they first become in any way conspicuous is a necessary and proper test of character and mettle. Those who cannot take it, or talk too much, or are

During this social week of racing and
parties there was plenty of opportunity for
Prince Andrew and Sarah to laugh and
talk together and the old friendship changed
into courtship. As Prince Andrew later
said, 'It was at Ascot that the whole thing
took off.'

found under relentless inspection to have blotted their reputation irretrievably, thereby become instantly ineligible. This seems to put an unexpected constitutional duty on the more enterprising popular papers, but a test of patience and ingenuity it certainly is. From that day at Ascot they could expect only gossip and headlines if they were found together. The thought alone must do something to a romance.

They had met each other from time to time since childhood, but, after Ascot, they seem to agree that they felt an increasing liking for each other. The Prince flew back from a short, official visit to Canada (New Brunswick, Nova Scotia and Ontario), on leave from the navy, on 13 July, and telephoned her at Clapham to invite her out for the evening. They had supper at Buckingham Palace and then went out dancing afterwards. They spent weekends with friends, among them Mr Nocon at Beaconsfield, the David Frosts at Arundel, and the Prince's old school friend Mr Alistair Hadden-Paton near Berkhamsted, in Hertfordshire. They spent a week together at Balmoral. She was asked to join the royal party at Sandringham in the New Year, after the royal family had spent Christmas together, as the Queen prefers, at Windsor. At Sandringham they were spotted out together, holding hands, which made up a number of minds as theirs, they say, had already been.

Two happenings in February seemed to confirm that the engagement was on the way – as indeed it was. The Princess of Wales and Prince William took Miss Ferguson on a family visit to the frigate HMS *Brazen*, and its officers and men, while the ship was on a four-day goodwill visit to London. It seemed quite a hint. Prince Andrew instructed her before the cameras: 'Keep smiling, for goodness sake.' She was getting used to it. Then she went off to Klosters, in Switzerland for a skiing holiday with the Prince and Princess of Wales. Most of the media's questions to her were fended off deftly, but the press reception for her when she arrived back at Heathrow airport on her own would have frightened anybody. Photographers kicked and punched each other and the police had to rescue her. Her car then failed to start. An airport worker said she had told him it was the longest five minutes of her life.

Prince Andrew and his girlfriend during a pheasant shoot at Sandringham. The Queen had invited Sarah to join the traditional New Year party in Norfolk. Wearing her distinctive Davy Crocket-style fur hat Sarah tramped across the fields with Prince Andrew and his labrador. By now the royal family knew for certain that the romance was indeed serious.

The Princess of Wales on board Prince Andrew's ship, HMS Brazen accompanied by Sarah. To the surprise and delight of the photographers waiting for the royal party, the Princess of Wales and Prince William were accompanied by Sarah when they toured the ship on its goodwill visit to London. The Princess of Wales guided her friend through the ordeal of facing the barrage of cameramen and the visit increased the speculation about an imminent royal engagement.

Two days after the visit to HMS Brazen Sarah joined the Prince and Princess of Wales on their skiing holiday in Klosters, Switzerland. Going up the mountain on the T-bar gave the Princess of Wales and her friend a few moments of conversation undisturbed by the hovering press.

Floors Castle, the Scottish home of the Duke and Duchess of Roxburghe. Prince Andrew has been a friend of the young couple for a long time and has spent many happy weekends there, shooting or fishing on the river. It was here in this eighteenth-century castle, the largest inhabited mansion in Britain, that he proposed formally to Sarah, on both knees, towards the end of February. Much to his surprise, she laughingly accepted.

Below: Miss Ferguson glowing with happiness on her engagement day, relieved that after the many weeks of pressure from the media she could openly show her feelings for Prince Andrew. The previous twenty-four hours had been a whirlwind of activity, including ordering the wool crêpe suit that she wore for the engagement interviews and photo-call.

Facing page: Prince Andrew and his fiancée during the engagement interview which took place in his second-floor study at Buckingham Palace. After the initial congratulations from the court correspondents the proud Princess-to-be showed off her diamond and ruby engagement ring. The ring, a fine oval Burma ruby with ten-drop diamonds set cluster-style and mounted in 18-carat white and yellow gold, had been made in great secrecy by the royal jewellers, Garrard to a design sketched by Prince Andrew. During the interview Miss Ferguson took umbridge when Prince Andrew lightheartedly described the craftsmen as 'very nice engineers'. Her relaxed approach to the announcement day gave the interview a freshness and spontaneity that delighted the nation.

On the weekend of 22-3 February it was all settled, bar telling the world, buying the dress and hiring the Abbey. The *Brazen* had docked at Sunderland. She flew north to Newcastle under an assumed name. They met at Floors Castle, the very extensive and stately home of their friends, the Duke and Duchess of Roxburghe. They had been there two years before, when they had found they enjoyed each other's company but still had other, more important interests. Now, by their own account given to Anthony Carthew of ITN and Michael Cole of BBC News in their engagement interview, he proposed to her formally. He did it on both knees, and she accepted (he said it surprised him), on the generous understanding that if he woke up in the morning thinking better of it, he could say it had all been a huge joke. He did not.

Royal engagement interviews are taking off as media events: they will be in the Court Circular yet. For the disrespectful they are an entertainment. For the less experienced of the participants they are an evident embarrassment. Both the Princess of Wales and Captain Mark Phillips had never known anything like it before and, once married, took care not

Miss Ferguson's mother, Mrs Hector Barrantes looking at photographs of her daughter's engagement in London which had been wired to Buenos Aires. During the winter months in London when she was under intense pressure from the media, Miss Ferguson had confided in her mother during many long-distance telephone calls to Argentina.

to submit themselves to interviewing again for some years. Among marriage devotees it helps to confirm who is supposed to be the dominant spouse (although it need not work out that way), and to bring out the details essential to a television romance. This time it came over clearly that the future Princess had a good tongue in her head.

It appeared that she also packs a punch. They had, according to the Prince, been 'made to sit next door to each other' at lunch on the famous day at Ascot. He had made her eat the chocolate profiteroles. She had been on a diet. So she hit him, and in his mother's presence too (she seems to have approved). So that was where true love began? He thought so: 'There are always humble beginnings. It's got to start somewhere.' It certainly made a change from the more sugary sort of royal recollection.

And, of course, the ring. This was the highlight. They had not had to go out to buy it; the jewellers (he, being a naval man, called them 'engineers') came in to ask them for suggestions, and he had helped in the design. She was naturally delighted with it: 'Stunning. Red. I wanted a ruby. Well, I didn't *want* it. I'm very lucky to have it. Certainly it's a lovely stone. I've got red hair too.' He let it be known that he had, properly, asked both the Queen's and Major Ferguson's approval. They had not thought about how many children they wanted. She said they were 'good friends, good team . . . very happy.' He said: 'We are both over the moon.'

There followed weeks of a steady accumulation of unofficial minutiae about her. Her musical taste runs to Beethoven and Mozart as well as to Jennifer Rush, Tina Turner and Elton John. It emerged that they had actually gone to an Elton John concert at Wembley before Christmas, and had held hands, but nobody had noticed. She supported Lady Theresa Manners's aristocratic pop group, The Business Connection. She likes Phil Collins and Duran Duran. They went to Covent Garden together to see the new punk-style ballet, *Frankenstein, the Modern*

Prometheus. She reads thrillers by John Le Carré, Frederick Forsyth and Len Deighton. She does aerobics. She is a strong swimmer. The experts said the ring must cost at least £25,000. She used to drive a blue BMW at high speeds, but after her engagement changed, tactfully, to a patriotic Jaguar XJS. She does not read newspapers much and gets her news from television. She and her flatmate did take *Harpers & Queen, The Tatler* and *Vogue,* as well-brought up young women tend to do. She does not like 'Dallas' or 'Dynasty'. Much of this appeared to the public to be highly reassuring.

Her friends are sure she will do well, that she will do everything to make a success for them both. They seem to feel, too, that the media have been mildly unfair in type-casting her so far as one of a cheerfully snobbish young set in SW3 and SW7 with better social connections than sense. Her old flatmate, Mrs Cotterell, says: 'Sarah will take her role as The Princess Andrew extremely seriously. She will perform it very well indeed.' Her former friend Mr McNally says: 'Any man would be lucky to marry her. She'll go far . . . very far.' Her mother says: 'She is twenty-six, but there is a much older and more mature head on her shoulders. She is not some silly slip of a girl, some dumb Sloane Ranger, even if her clothes and her appearance might make some people think she is.' What she is, beyond doubt, is a young woman of her times. She has the makings of someone who may turn out to do pretty well for her times.

Miss Ferguson holding her baby half-sister, Eliza Ferguson on her christening day at Dummer Down Farm in March. Prince Charles agreed to be one of the baby's godparents, thus cementing further the links between the two families.

HRH Princess Andrew's descent
from King James I

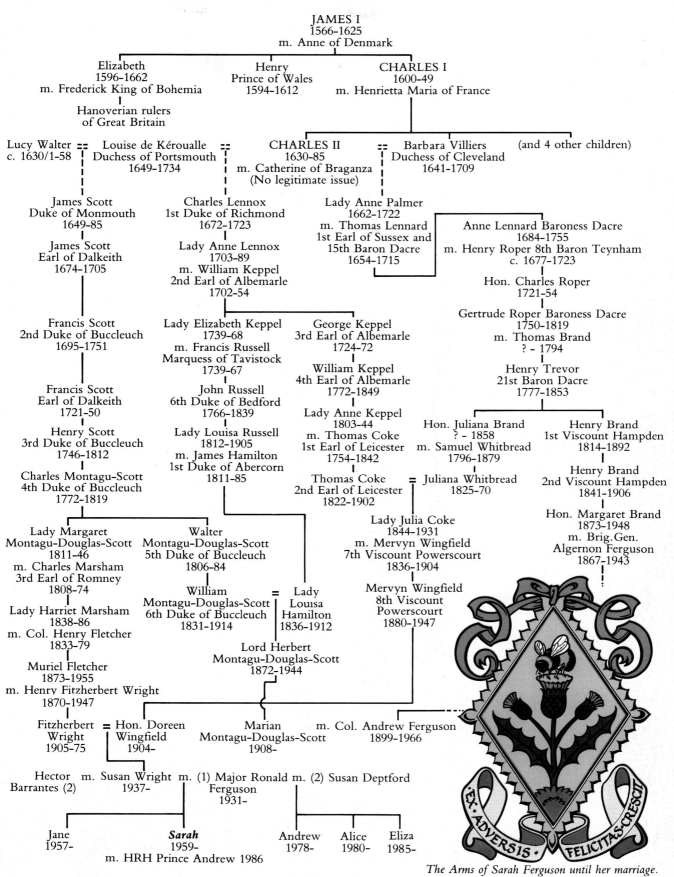

JAMES I
1566–1625
m. Anne of Denmark

Elizabeth
1596–1662
m. Frederick King of Bohemia

Hanoverian rulers
of Great Britain

Henry
Prince of Wales
1594–1612

CHARLES I
1600–49
m. Henrietta Maria of France

Lucy Walter
c. 1630/1-58

Louise de Kéroualle
Duchess of Portsmouth
1649–1734

CHARLES II
1630–85
m. Catherine of Braganza
(No legitimate issue)

Barbara Villiers
Duchess of Cleveland
1641–1709

(and 4 other children)

James Scott
Duke of Monmouth
1649–85

Charles Lennox
1st Duke of Richmond
1672–1723

Lady Anne Palmer
1662–1722
m. Thomas Lennard
1st Earl of Sussex and
15th Baron Dacre
1654–1715

Anne Lennard Baroness Dacre
1684–1755
m. Henry Roper 8th Baron Teynham
c. 1677–1723

James Scott
Earl of Dalkeith
1674–1705

Lady Anne Lennox
1703–89
m. William Keppel
2nd Earl of Albemarle
1702–54

Hon. Charles Roper
1721–54

Francis Scott
2nd Duke of Buccleuch
1695–1751

Lady Elizabeth Keppel
1739–68
m. Francis Russell
Marquess of Tavistock
1739–67

George Keppel
3rd Earl of Albemarle
1724–72

Gertrude Roper Baroness Dacre
1750–1819
m. Thomas Brand
? – 1794

Francis Scott
Earl of Dalkeith
1721–50

John Russell
6th Duke of Bedford
1766–1839

William Keppel
4th Earl of Albemarle
1772–1849

Henry Trevor
21st Baron Dacre
1777–1853

Henry Scott
3rd Duke of Buccleuch
1746–1812

Lady Louisa Russell
1812–1905
m. James Hamilton
1st Duke of Abercorn
1811–85

Lady Anne Keppel
1803–44
m. Thomas Coke
1st Earl of Leicester
1754–1842

Hon. Juliana Brand
? – 1858
m. Samuel Whitbread
1796–1879

Henry Brand
1st Viscount Hampden
1814–1892

Charles Montagu-Scott
4th Duke of Buccleuch
1772–1819

Thomas Coke
2nd Earl of Leicester
1822–1902

Juliana Whitbread
1825–70

Henry Brand
2nd Viscount Hampden
1841–1906

Lady Margaret
Montagu-Douglas-Scott
1811–46
m. Charles Marsham
3rd Earl of Romney
1808–74

Walter
Montagu-Douglas-Scott
5th Duke of Buccleuch
1806–84

Lady Julia Coke
1844–1931
m. Mervyn Wingfield
7th Viscount Powerscourt
1836–1904

Hon. Margaret Brand
1873–1948
m. Brig.Gen.
Algernon Ferguson
1867–1943

Lady Harriet Marsham
1838–86
m. Col. Henry Fletcher
1833–79

William
Montagu-Douglas-Scott
6th Duke of Buccleuch
1831–1914

Lady
Louisa
Hamilton
1836–1912

Mervyn Wingfield
8th Viscount
Powerscourt
1880–1947

Muriel Fletcher
1873–1955
m. Henry Fitzherbert Wright
1870–1947

Lord Herbert
Montagu-Douglas-Scott
1872–1944

Fitzherbert
Wright
1905–75

Hon. Doreen
Wingfield
1904–

Marian
Montagu-Douglas-Scott
1908–

m. Col. Andrew Ferguson
1899–1966

Hector
Barrantes (2)

m. Susan Wright
1937–

m. (1) Major Ronald
Ferguson
1931–

m. (2) Susan Deptford

Jane
1957–

Sarah
1959–
m. HRH Prince Andrew 1986

Andrew
1978–

Alice
1980–

Eliza
1985–

EX · ADVERSIS · FELICITAS · CRESCIT

The Arms of Sarah Ferguson until her marriage.

73

ROYAL MARRIAGES

ROYAL weddings came late into the limelight. Though they are now essential to the popularity of the royal family, indispensable to its devotees across the world, and especially so to the media, they were held in private for centuries (often for very good reason) and late at night. It was not just that the energetic Edward IV wedded and bedded Elizabeth Woodville in such secrecy that he did not dare to tell his own council for five months that he had hitched himself to a commoner, or that Anne Boleyn was pregnant when she married Henry VIII, or that he was nearly as furtive about another wife, Catherine Howard (the big show in town that day was the execution of Thomas Cromwell); simplicity, if not actual surreptitiousness, was the thing.

Charles II, with some reason, was casual about weddings. He was married in Portsmouth, of all places, and was not at his best for the unfortunate Catherine of Braganza, confessing afterwards: 'I was happy for the honour of the nation that I was not put to the consummation of the marriage last night; for I was so sleepy by having slept but two hours in my journey as I was afraid that matters would have gone very sleepily.'

His brother, the Duke of York who briefly became James II and VII, kept his first marriage to Anne Hyde, mother of the future Mary II and Queen Anne, a complete secret as long as he could. Mary herself was

married in her own bedchamber at St James's Palace at 9 pm to Prince William of Orange. When King Charles heard William promising to endow her with all his worldly goods, he told his niece loudly: 'Put it all up in your pocket, for 'tis clear gain.' The remark was not appreciated. So, marrying her sister Anne to Prince George of Denmark at the Chapel Royal, St James's, in 1683 he insisted that there should be neither ceremony nor ostentation.

Princess Charlotte, on the evening she arrived from Mecklenberg to marry George III in 1761, was promptly put into a dress she had never seen before, and the service again took place at 9 pm. When the wedding-day of her granddaughter Princess Charlotte came, the girl simply had dinner with the old queen and her aunts before driving swiftly to Carlton House. Perhaps it was as well that the service was private, for the royal bride shared Charles II's idea of a joke. She laughed out loud at the moment the impoverished Prince Leopold repeated: 'With all my worldly goods I thee endow.' But then the views of her father, George IV, about marriage were nothing if not antipathetic.

Above: Queen Victoria's wedding to Prince Albert of Saxe-Coburg-Gotha took place on a rainy day in February 1840 in the Chapel Royal, St James's.

When Prince of Wales he married Caroline of Brunswick in 1795 to try to persuade the Commons to pay off his debts. On seeing his bride he said, in a well-publicized aside: 'I am not well. Pray get me a brandy.' He was drunk throughout the proceedings.

It was Queen Victoria who made the first, small concession to public curiosity because the public was interested in her, a personable and innocent young woman, as it had not been in her disreputable uncles. What is more, she was genuinely in love. On her wedding morning, 10 February 1840, a Monday, she wrote a quick note to her Albert, who was staying a couple of corridors away in Buckingham Palace:

Dearest, how are you today and have you slept well? What weather! I believe, however, the rain will cease. Send one word when you, my most dearly beloved bridegroom, will be ready.
 Thy every faithful,
 Victoria.

The Queen very much wanted the marriage to be a success, and all the more because *The Times*, which was in itself all the media of the day that mattered, was sardonic about the Queen and her intended. The newspaper did not approve of Prince Albert, wishing him to have been 'a person of riper years, and likely to form more sound and circumspect opinion than this youth, however promising, of twenty-one.' But it felt sorry for him, too, condemned to her Whig court in which 'the well-educated German prince . . . should not be able to discover within reach of him a single companion capable of carrying on a conversation with him on any subject more elevated than a fox-hunt, a field day or a battue.'

So Queen Victoria was married at noon, though her drive was only a short one from Buckingham Palace to the Chapel Royal, St James's, just down the road. The weather was wet and there was little for people to see. The windows of Prince Albert's carriage were closed, so he was scarcely recognized. Florence Nightingale said, stuffily, Prince Albert was dressed in 'clothes which no doubt he borrowed to be married in.' The longest cheer of all was for the famous Duke of Wellington, one of only five Tories invited. But despite the rain the populace turned up. Boys were reported to have fallen out of trees trying to get a proper view. They did not, however, catch her quizzical look, copying her cousin, Princess Charlotte when Prince Albert duly promised to endow her with his worldly goods. It was getting to be a standard bit of business.

Still the Queen did agree to obey him and wept twice, and the crowds were still there when they drove off, as Greville, a famous diarist of the period, said, 'in a very poor and shabby style . . . in one of the old travelling coaches, the postillions in undressed liveries,' for their brief honeymoon at Windsor. She found the loyal reception en route 'most enthusiastic and hearty and gratifying in every way,' but she did not like being out of London for more than three days: 'You forget, my dearest love, that I am the Sovereign.'

When Queen Victoria's eldest daughter, the Princess Royal, was married to the Crown Prince of Prussia on 25 January 1858, it, too, took place at St James's, in the chapel that *The Times* said was 'not much larger than the principal apartment of a catacomb.' Outside, it felt the crowds were badly done by:

They were a sight greater than that they came to see. But to look on these hundreds of thousands, and to consider how little they saw of what affected to be a pageant, and how little they were allowed to share in what was a national celebration, could not but excite a painful feeling.

The chapel was not big enough for even an ordinary society wedding. The processional route was the shortest possible. Few of those who turned up could see the carriages and horses. Queen Victoria seems to have sensed the disappointment herself. Having returned to the Palace, she opened the window to the balcony and brought her daughter and the Crown Prince out to be seen and applauded. To her goes the credit for inventing what has become the essential royal wedding picture. It was so unexpected that the *Times* man missed it.

The middle-class demand to see its royal family grew apace with the spread of the new newspapers in London and throughout the provinces after the abolition of the newspaper stamp. The bourgeois circulations had to be fed by fine writing on great spectacle, and the new electric telegraph made sure they were not disappointed. So when Queen Victoria moved out to Windsor and seclusion on Prince Albert's death, she met more popular dissatisfaction at her withdrawal, however loyally expressed, than she (and her predecessors) might have had reason to expect.

She did not even try to put things right at the Prince of Wales's wedding at St George's Chapel, Windsor, in 1863. She flatly ignored the advice that the Abbey or St Paul's would be more appropriate for the wedding of her eldest son, though the last royal wedding at St George's Chapel had been Henry I's second marriage to Adeliza of Louvain in 1122. (He had been hoping for an heir to replace the one that went down in the White Ship, but he was unlucky.) But it happened that the Prince of Wales's wedding was prefaced by an extraordinary drive through London by Princess Alexandra of Denmark and her father beforehand, which brought the crowds and the reporters out in droves. There were 12,000 people on special scaffolding outside St Paul's alone. This drive, however, had not been Victoria's intention and it had happened because the Danish royal party, travelling from Sheerness by the South-Eastern Railway, had to get out at the Bricklayers' Arms terminal and drive five miles across London to catch the train for Windsor at Paddington.

The streets were packed, even though there were complaints that London had no great processional way (and was not to have one until the Mall and Admiralty Arch were finished just before the First World War), the royal carriages on duty were old and shabby and the horses were thought very poor, with no trappings, not even rosettes, and no out-riders. *Punch* declared that the wedding was being held 'in an obscure Berkshire village, noted only for an old castle with bad drains.' Nor was the new technology much good. There were photographers at the wedding, but they were employed by the artist, Frith, to record for him the features and gestures he did not have time to sketch: most of the plates did not come out, and he had to go begging for later sittings by the great and good.

It was all very well for Walter Bagehot, the constitutionalist, to insist that 'the women – one half the human race at least – care fifty times more for a marriage than a ministry', the Queen would not change her mind. Actually, it turned out that too many of Victoria's children had a

The wedding of the Prince of Wales, later Edward VII, to Princess Alexandra of Denmark was held at St George's Chapel, Windsor in March 1863. Queen Victoria was still in deep mourning for her husband, Prince Albert and refused to travel to London for the wedding. The Queen, wearing her widow's weeds, watched the ceremony from the gallery in the Chapel.

propensity for unhappy marriages, so she may have been wise not to make too much of them. The marriage she probably preferred was her youngest child, Princess Beatrice's to Prince Henry Maurice of Battenberg, on 23 July 1885, which the Queen insisted should be held at Whippingham parish church, close to her home, Osborne House on the Isle of Wight. It meant that all the 'swells', including the Prince of Wales, had to cross by ferry from Portsmouth at an early hour of the morning, but the old Queen was so pleased by the marriage that she gave the bride away herself.

A marriage that excited both royalty and press alike was the wedding of the Duke of York (later George V) to Princess May of Teck on 6 July

1893. The route from Buckingham Palace to St James's was extended to Piccadilly and St James's Street, and though the day was not even a bank holiday (arousing suspicions, not for the last time, that officialdom took pleasure in the contrast between the popular enthusiasm and its own apathy), the trees in the parks were filled again with youthful spectators and clubmen gathered at the windows in St James's to watch the procession. What mattered most was that the Duke of York loved Sandringham above all places on earth, and insisted on honeymooning there in the ghastly little house, York Cottage, that his bride soon came to hate. To reach Sandringham the bridal pair had to travel by train from Liverpool Street, and to get to Liverpool Street there had to be a lengthy ceremonial carriage drive, past St Paul's, where the City again put up stands, and where the couple stopped to receive the congratulations of the Lord Mayor and Sheriffs. Satin slippers and rice were thrown freely. The train stopped in Cambridge for an official address, so they were dead beat by the time they reached Norfolk. Meanwhile in London, gas jets, electric lights and fairy lamps lit up the West End with decorations, loyal messages and other illuminations for the wandering, and occasionally illuminated, crowds.

The memory of the day's success must have remained with George V because, when the next generation's turn came to get married, he decided on an experiment. Princess Patricia of Connaught ('Princess Pat'), the immensely capable and popular daughter of the Duke of Connaught, was to marry a commoner, Commander Alexander Ramsay RN. The First World War had been over for just three months. The empires of continental Europe, the Habsburgs, the Hohenzollerns, the Romanovs, had been swept away. It seemed an apt time to put on a royal show to entertain London, if not the one surviving Empire.

So the wedding was held at Westminster Abbey on 27 February 1919. Everyone knew the Abbey because of two recent coronations, but no one, not even the Dean and Chapter, could remember when a wedding had ever been held there. In the end it was thought that Richard II and Anne of Bohemia had been the last to get married there in the fourteenth century, but there were historical doubts about this; in fact, the last confirmed one was that of Edmund Crouchback, second son of Henry II, to Aveline, heiress of the wealthy Earl of Albemarle in the twelfth century. It had been that long ago. Precisely what prompted George V's bit of showmanship is not plain, but the man who had staged the Delhi Durbar in 1911 was no slouch at public pageantry and its uses. The wedding suddenly caught the public's imagination, and put royal weddings at the Abbey (and at St Paul's five years ago) into the public-relations calendar from then on.

It was the *Daily Mail* (still calling itself The Soldiers' Paper) that probably put its finger on it. It was glad, it said, that it was a love match because 'it is comparatively rarely that princesses follow the dictate of their heart' but, much more than that, the real break with the past was that it was a properly patriotic, overtly British wedding. There was no need now for the princelings and serene highnesses that had taken over royal celebrations in Queen Victoria's time. The bridegroom was a navy man, so he was still a hero; the bride had helped to raise her own regiment, Princess Patricia's Canadian Light Infantry, in August 1914. It was a unique chance to celebrate the victory all over again, and with it the success of the recently renamed House of Windsor:

Throughout the Empire the decision to avoid the German taint has been received with approval. The war showed how subtle and far-reaching the influence of German manners and traditions could be, and nothing pleased the British peoples better than the King's action in banning this influence and breaking with it finally.

So the crowds that turned out on the way to the Abbey were enormous, almost embarrassingly so for so junior a member of the family. They stopped cars and taxis and stood on the roofs to have a better view; they stood on the captured German tanks on show at Horse Guards; soldiers climbed the statues in Parliament Square. Pickpockets had a field day. All this for a landau with a girl who was about to give up her title and retire from royal life. As the honeymoon car left Clarence House the crush was so great that it was forced to a stop in the Mall. It was, beyond question, the start of something big.

George V was the begetter of the democratic monarchy. After all, he was the monarch who agreed to create 1,000 peers to force the hand of the Tory House of Lords. He picked a Conservative prime minister from the Commons, not the Lords, in 1923. And he welcomed the first, minority Labour government in 1924 (although he wondered in his diary what his grandmother would have thought about that). He got the message from 'Princess Pat's' day. So his own children began to be married at the Abbey.

The wedding group of the Duke and Duchess of York, later King George VI and Queen Mary, in July 1893. The Duke who was second-in-line to the throne, made a popular choice of bride, Princess May of Teck, an English Princess.

First came Princess Mary, the only daughter he doted on, marrying an older and unremarkable Yorkshire landowner, Viscount Lascelles, a friend of her father's, on 28 February 1922. The popular newspapers promptly went to town. The *Daily Mail*, its circulation now topping 1.5 million, kept to a winning line: 'The charm of this match is it leaves no taste of scheming dynastic politics. It is just an English girl and an Englishman who have fallen in love with each other.'

The *Express* was verbally more adventurous: 'Our Fairy Princess Married', it announced with evident satisfaction and, drawing on her auxiliary nursing experience in the First World War, called her 'the little white heroine of the nation'. And Beaverbrook, the *Express*'s redoubtable owner, was not taking lessons in popular patriotism from anyone, either: 'There were no glittering crowds of foreign potentates. Formality and the cold glamour of thrones that rest on bayonets was not there.'

The essential miscellany of the trousseau was discussed for weeks on end. The wedding dress was exhibited to the loyal press by the manufacturers, in a glass case (a service now withheld for greater theatrical effect on the day). So were her shoes, her going-away hat, and even the wedding cake itself. This was a full-dress show. The procession passed through Admiralty Arch to Trafalgar Square and down Whitehall. Six thousand police were on duty. The railway companies ran excursions from the provinces; the London and South-West Railway even issued cheap tickets in Paris, where it found bookings were 'exceptionally heavy'.

So many people crowded into Trafalgar Square that the police could not contain them. They broke through the line and swept down Whitehall, where they refused to budge, leaving only a narrow path for the coaches, into whose windows they stared with a sense of happy achievement. When the service was over there was a queue two miles long just to see inside the Abbey where the nobility and beauty of the land had been. Back at the Palace the bride's appearance on the balcony was the first by the royal family since Armistice Day.

And now new media were getting into the act. The film cameras were there for the wedding procession, though not for the service. Film was flown to Leeds (the centre for the Lascelles country) that night and the cinemas stayed open after 11 pm to enable people to see it. Next day Harrods showed a half-hour film of the procession and other events in the Princess's life from 11 am to 5.30 pm. The new wireless just managed to make itself heard. The Princess's wedding music was 'radiated by wireless telephone' by the Marconi company (call sign 2MT). There were thought to have been only 7,000 amateur enthusiasts around London with apparatus capable of receiving the Marconi transmission. In the United States the trousseau was photographed for the front page of the New York *World*. Duplicates of the wedding dress were instantly on sale in Fifth Avenue. This was just another part of the royal story that was going to run and run.

Almost unnoticed by the newspapers had been one of Princess Mary's eight bridesmaids, who shared her interest in the Girl Guides and was now a rising name in London society: Lady Elizabeth Bowes-Lyon. But that obscurity promptly ended in January 1923, when her engagement was announced to the Duke of York, George V's second son, whom the family called Bertie. The stage was set for the emergence of the most popular royal actress of the century. Nothing could fail on 26 April, her wedding day. Over a million people lined the streets of London, the hardiest of them standing in the rain outside Buckingham Palace from 6 am. There were 7,000 police – and 3,000 casualties beset by the usual royal enthusiasts' ailments. The *Daily Telegraph,* thoughtfully, regretted that 'only a relatively small company will be privileged to witness the solemn ceremony at Westminster'. Not, apparently, trusting the professional skills of its own picture department it sympathized with the many spectators who would be 'only a meagre minority of those who would be in the happy arena today if they could'. At least it was able to illustrate the bridal gown that morning.

The *Daily Mail* (1d, and now claiming the 'World's Largest Net Daily Sale') and the *Daily Mirror* had no doubts about how to splash it all. The *Mirror,* a month after a special edition celebrating the diamond jubilee of Queen Alexandra, then the Queen Mother, landing on British soil sixty years before ('How She Has Won The Love Of The Whole Nation'), devoted over half its pages to the wedding, nine of them photographs, four of them text, and proudly claimed that its readers got them 'even in remote Ireland and Scotland'. The London *Evening News* had twenty-seven pictures in its late extra edition (no mean feat at that time) and a special fast aircraft was brought in from Belgium to fly pictures north to the *Mail*'s Manchester plant. Indeed, the first aircraft to leave London for the Irish Free State (as it was then called) since its inception carried press photographs for the republicans of Dublin.

The Times was patronizing, not unusually, about the bride. People, it said, 'know very little about her, as of necessity they know very little about well-bred young ladies living quietly at home, but all they do know is good and commendable.' Just as percipiently, it added: 'There is one wedding to which they look forward with still deeper interest – the wedding which will give a wife to the Heir to the Throne, and, in the course of nature, a future queen to England and to the British peoples'.

The wedding group of George V's only daughter, Princess Mary, later the Princess Royal, who married Viscount Lascelles in February 1922 at Westminster Abbey. Lady Elizabeth Bowes-Lyon was one of the bridesmaids (back row, second from the left); she would be a royal bride herself just fifteen months later.

An austere wedding photograph of the Duke and Duchess of York, later King George VI and Queen Elizabeth, now the Queen Mother, in the Throne Room at Buckingham Palace. This was the first time that a son of a British king had married a commoner instead of someone who was royal in her own right.

George V had long had much the same idea, although even then he was probably beginning to doubt it.

The bride rode with her father, the Earl of Strathmore in a coach with the Strathmore arms on it from their London home at 17 Bruton Street (now demolished) and the sun came out for her, which was held to be mildly miraculous. At the Abbey, Winston Churchill was late. The bride left her white handbag behind, and it had to be recovered quickly. One of the clergy fainted, and in the delay the bride showed her flair for the occasion by quietly placing her bouquet beside the Tomb of the Unknown Warrior. She returned with her new husband in the Glass Coach, the better to be seen. On the Palace balcony later she was bold enough to throw a kiss to the crowds below.

That evening the radio again did its best for its small but enthusiastic audience. (One of the most remarked-on presents installed in the royal couple's future home at White Lodge, Richmond Park, was 'a valve apparatus capable of picking up signals from distant stations' – from an admirer in New York.) In London at 7 pm the Choir of Westminster Abbey turned up to repeat the wedding anthem for all of ten minutes. Up in loyal Newcastle the Wireless Orchestra played Mendelssohn's Wedding March in the same slot. Birmingham and Manchester offered their listeners no such flourishes. Back at the Abbey the Dean and Chapter were charging one shilling (5p) to the queues up from the suburbs who wanted to see everything for themselves. Hastily-processed news film was shown that night around England south of the Tyne and in South Wales. The royal extravaganza was on the road.

It was also happening in the United States. The good, grey *New York Times* previewed the wedding on its front page, in a single-column report 'by wireless', introducing what it called a 'modest little Scotch girl . . . Britain's most talked-of and most envied girl'. It promptly did more than most British papers dared by pointing out, in its second paragraph: 'Unless the Prince of Wales marries and has issue, his presumptive successors to the throne will be the Duke of York and any issue of the present marriage'.

That was telling them. Next day the newspaper went to town with the marriage headings in the style it has made its own:

DUKE OF YORK WEDS SIMPLE SCOTS MAID
Little Bride Appears Overwhelmed – King
Greets Her With Hearty Kiss
MAN WITH A RED FLAG HUSTLED BY CROWD

Understandably unknowing of what the little bride was going to mean to the monarchy, the *New York Times* man played up the Cinderella angle:

It was a very nervous girl who bowed shyly as she passed through the crowds that lined the way to the Abbey . . . She was bowing, but it was a timid, nervous bow. She was grateful for their greeting – she wanted to acknowledge it, but she seemed to be half-frightened by all this demonstration for her. . . .

She curtsied low to her husband's royal parents, but the King, with smiling gallantry, bent low and raised the blushing girl, saying 'Come, Your Royal Highness'.

There was no follow-up as to what happened to the man with the red flag.

The wedding in 1934 of Princess Marina of Greece and Prince George, newly created Duke of Kent, was a popular one and the bride delighted London with her elegance and Continental chic. By now royal marriages in Westminster Abbey had become public spectacles.

Facing page: Princess Elizabeth and Prince Philip photographed by Baron in the Throne Room at Buckingham Palace after their wedding at Westminster Abbey in November 1947. This was the first ceremonial occasion of any splendour after the years of war austerity. The public had sent in clothing coupons to help the bride pay for her magnificently embroidered dress.

George V was robbed, partly to his own relief, of the wedding spectacular he had once wished for by the evident reluctance of his eldest son to marry, but the Duke of Kent's marriage to Princess Marina of Greece on 29 November 1934, went off spectacularly well, even though London was so foggy Admiralty Arch could not be seen from Buckingham Palace. The authorities still gave the newspapers advance details of the dresses, and even of the bouquet. Half a million people came into London from the provinces, and 30,000 from abroad. They were rewarded by an unusually elegant royal bride, who had sensibly picked her clothes in Paris, and by the sight of Princess Elizabeth, then only eight, stoutly doing her duty as a bridesmaid and holding the train up as high as her own eyeline. Her sister, Princess Margaret Rose, was still thought too small and sat on a stool in the Abbey beside her mother. Later, the King himself held her up on the Palace balcony to see and be seen.

This was the first wedding when radio made an impact. Two commentators, Mr Howard Marshall and an Austrian, broadcast what was called 'a running description' to most of the sets in the world. The programme ran from 10.45 am to 12 pm on the National programme, pleased a delighted public, and was heard in both Australia and Canada. The wireless was entering its great age, in which it would, almost effortlessly, come to scoop both the newsreels and colour magazines. It was live. It brought the great occasions directly into the living-rooms

and kitchens of the English-speaking countries. George V had encouraged it by his Christmas broadcasts to the Empire, in which his voice, grandfatherly, reassuring, patently sincere, came over so well that it was the photograph of the King at the microphone, and not of the King with the crown on his head, that became the accepted image of the democratic monarchy.

The abdication message of Edward VIII in December 1936 added drama and perturbation to royal broadcasting, so much so that the American radio networks arranged to carry it by short-wave from 5 pm; 300 stations picked up the signal from London and got what was called an 'unprecedented' audience. In turn, the Coronation of George VI the following May had an audience of 300 million people worldwide (and 50,000 in Britain on television); the American radio coverage, of almost seven hours, was the longest continuous programme the country had known. In under a decade radio had made the British monarchy the first one known directly in people's homes everywhere: and television was coming fast. 'What are the roads of Rome compared with this?' an American critic asked, 'or the telegraph and the airplane?'

Ten years later, after the worldwide destruction of the Second World War, radio and film had their finest, almost unchallenged, hour at the wedding of Princess Elizabeth to Lieutenant Philip Mountbatten, newly-created Duke of Edinburgh, at the Abbey on 20 November 1947. After two years of disappointed post-war expectations, the British had something to be pleased about and to do well, and to take them out of austerity for a day. Coaches were found, and uniforms for the Life Guards. The public sent in clothing coupons for the bride's dress. They meant to have a day to remember. That was how it seemed on both sides of the Atlantic. The three American networks pooled their coverage for a two-hour live broadcast beginning at 6 am. The *New York Times* made it its lead:

ELIZABETH AND PHILIP WED IN ABBEY
Worn, Shabby Britons Thrill to
Cavalry, Bands, Coaches

It devoted five pages and eleven pictures to tell the story, and one short paragraph to deliver the message:

So Britain had its holiday and went back to work. It went back to one egg or less a week, two ounces of butter a week, one quart of milk a week. . . . It went back to drabness and austerity, hard work and no glittering expectations; to the realization that the days of empire had passed.

Nine kings (not all of them still on their thrones) attended the wedding. The Poet Laureate, John Masefield, wrote of a crown idyllically set above greed and hate:

> To such a crown all broken spirits turn;
> And we, who see this young face passing by,
> See her as symbol of a power eterne,
> And pray that heaven bless her till she die.

Those given first-aid rose to 2,500, of whom forty had to be sent to hospital. Radio was allowed inside the Abbey. After all, it had done well in the war; it was trusted. Now it got its reward. The ceremony was broadcast in forty-two languages. But, like the film cameramen, it was about to be decisively overtaken as the chief communicator of royalty. Television was not in the Abbey, though the BBC's cameras were out in the streets of London for two and a half hours, on trial. The BBC sent its signal out to people within a sixty-mile radius of the transmitter, but that was all then, and for six years seemed likely to be all that the old guard would be prepared to allow. When Queen Mary died in 1953 her funeral procession from Marlborough House was televised for only half an hour. Television had to take radio sound for the service proper at Westminster Hall.

It was only at the last moment before the Queen's Coronation in June 1953 that television was accepted at the service; then the camerawork and Richard Dimbleby's commentary immediately gave the new reign a triumphant start around the world. Television had come of age over-night. The weddings of Princess Margaret in May 1960 and Princess Anne in November 1973, both at the Abbey, and of the Prince and Princess of Wales at St Paul's in July 1981, have seen the television audiences soar, so that 700 million people is now a routine estimate. From the days when air forces and airlines vied with each other to race film across the Atlantic to the age of the satellite, the curiosity and the demands of the international audiences have grown, and all the more so as state visits, and the unremitting informal ones, have continued the Windsor family's steady reconquest of the United States.

Before the Prince and Princess of Wales's wedding ABC's Peter Jennings and Barbara Walters broadcast a one-hour special programme from London to the United States. On the day itself there was wall-to-wall coverage from early dawn onwards. The American networks sent their best anchor people to London; they vied with the British for the best camera positions along the route (they are still, for the present anyway, excluded from the Abbey); and they and their audiences voted it all a success, and money well spent. A papal coronation apart, there is no other institution in the world that would be given such attention and respect.

Equally, the newspapers of much of the world have kept determinedly in the game. The imagery and the imaginations of their best headline writers and reporters make fortunes for their proprietors as well as excite and console their readers. The conjecture and the gossip about Prince Andrew and Miss Sarah Ferguson, not to mention their daily photographs, consumed countless acres of forest – all, of course, in the essential duty of cheering us all up. It has been a popular wedding because press and people wanted it to be popular.

It may be that what has happened with television is that the watching world can enjoy both the symbolism of the wedding and the sense of being at, of joining, a very private family occasion. It is not at all private in reality (only royal christenings and some royal funerals remain that). But for a moment disbelief and the real world are suspended, and those who wish to can return to the beliefs and hopes they once invested in marriage themselves. It is not by chance that the highest soap opera ratings are won by marriages. But that is not the real world at all. In a royal wedding there is enough reality, the continuing sense that the two people will lead real lives afterwards, for the very suspension of disbelief to be something rare and therefore the more enjoyable.

The twentieth-century monarchy has adapted itself, with only a few hiccups, to modern times, modern ways. It has had political help. It was

Princess Anne and Captain Mark Phillips photographed by Norman Parkinson at Buckingham Palace after their wedding at Westminster Abbey in November 1973.

Above: The Prince of Wales on his way to St Paul's Cathedral to marry Lady Diana Spencer in July 1981. He was accompanied by Prince Andrew wearing the uniform of a naval midshipman. At the wedding ceremony Prince Andrew acted as joint supporter with Prince Edward. At his own wedding this role was performed by Prince Edward alone.

Facing page: The last royal wedding was that of the Prince and Princess of Wales. Prince Charles decided in favour of St Paul's Cathedral rather than the more customary Westminster Abbey because of the longer processional route from Buckingham Palace and the large number of overseas guests invited to the wedding of the Heir to the Throne.

Lloyd George who dreamed up the idea of a public ceremony investing the Prince of Wales in 1911, the first of the sort for 300 years. He was not averse to the distraction of Princess Mary's wedding in February 1922. The day before it, he had actually written offering to step down as prime minister because his post-war coalition was falling apart. The Attlee government encouraged Princess Elizabeth's wedding in 1947: it did briefly cheer up a cheerless winter. Politicians never mind a circus or two, although royal circuses did not help Baldwin before his first election in 1923 or Heath in November 1973, before his trial of strength with the miners.

What would have been most remarkable to many people at the start of the century would have been the elevation of royal weddings, in little over sixty years, to a spectacle second only to a coronation. It would have surprised the court, which considered such occasions its own property. It would have surprised the earnest socialists just as much to find the weddings apparently so universally popular. In 1922, F. W. Jowett, then chairman of the Labour party, found it all too much a part of the class war: 'It is this class which gives us the spectacles of senseless and wasteful display at race meetings, royal levées, and royal weddings, hunting and shooting parties, and the gatherings of the swell mob at continental pleasure resorts.'

The sentiment is not exactly unknown now. But after 23 July it is a bold man who does not think royal weddings have come to stay. The alliance of crown, people and media has seen to that.

The Queen's Sixtieth Birthday

Prince Andrew and Miss Ferguson accompanied the Queen when she appeared on the balcony of Buckingham Palace to acknowledge the tributes of 6,000 children who walked down the Mall bearing over 120,000 golden daffodils. The royal party then descended to the Palace forecourt to meet the children and listen to their singing.

Facing page: That evening the royal family, including Miss Ferguson, turned out in force for the gala at the Royal Opera House, Covent Garden. Miss Ferguson wore a full-length royal blue, black and cream satin, off-the-shoulder gown for her first royal evening engagement.

Facing page and left: Miss Ferguson joined the Queen and other members of the royal family at this year's Royal Windsor Horse Show which takes place in May in Windsor Great Park. A keen rider herself, she watched the equestrian events with interest and did not seem to mind the unseasonal weather.

Below left: Even in the wind and rain at a polo match at Smith's Lawn, Windsor Miss Ferguson's charm shines through. It was her sparkling manner and infectious smile on such informal occasions that first captivated Prince Andrew.

Below right: Miss Ferguson's first official engagement with Prince Andrew took place in early June at the Pavilion Theatre in Weymouth. The gala night of old time music hall songs was in aid of King George's Fund for Sailors.

Facing page: Prince Charles greeting his future sister-in-law at a polo match in June. Prince Charles has known the Ferguson family for many years.

Left: Perfect partners at a charity clay pigeon shoot in early June. Prince Andrew is an expert shot and this year, he had his fiancée as his loader.

Below left: For Trooping the Colour this year, the royal party included Miss Ferguson for the first time.

Below: Prince Andrew and Miss Ferguson at the Imperial War Museum's display of aircraft at Duxford, Cambridgeshire.

Far below: After Trooping the Colour Miss Ferguson, along with other members of the royal family, attended the wedding of Miss Jane Gilmour to Peter Pleydell-Bouverie.

The Royal Meeting in June at Ascot is the highlight of the English summer season, both as a sporting occasion and as a social one with the elegant fashions, especially on Ladies' Day, attracting almost as much attention as the famous thoroughbred horses. This year Miss Ferguson delighted the crowds with her eyecatching dresses and hats.

Above: Princess Anne and Miss Ferguson drive up the course before the start of the afternoon's racing.

Left: After the racing is over, the royal party proceeds to Smith's Lawn to watch the polo.

Facing page above left: The Queen making her way through the Royal Enclosure followed by Miss Ferguson.

Above right: Prince Andrew accompanying his fiancée at Ascot.

Below: Miss Ferguson sitting next to Princess Michael of Kent for the carriage procession up the course.

Facing page: Prince Andrew and Miss Ferguson at the annual Schneider trophy air race, the world's longest closed circuit air event, on the Isle of Wight.

Above left: Miss Ferguson being helped on board the Navy patrol vessel HMS Cygnet by Royal Marine commandos during a surprise two-day visit to Northern Ireland.

Above right: In Northern Ireland she accompanied Prince Andrew on a series of engagements and the happy couple were welcomed with rousing cheers wherever they went.

Right: Miss Ferguson at the wedding of her former flatmate, Miss Carolyn Beckwith-Smith to Mr Harry Cotterell which took place in early July.

Below: Watching the tennis at Wimbledon with Carolyn Beckwith-Smith.

THE WEDDING

EVERYONE wanted the day to be a success – and it was. The Queen got it right; she created the bridegroom Duke of York, Earl of Inverness and Baron Killyeagh just ninety minutes before the wedding service. Her father and mother had also been Duke and Duchess of York, a title traditionally held by the Sovereign's second son, and she, too, had been Princess Elizabeth of York in her early years. So it was an indication of trust in her second son.

And the new Duke and Duchess of York got it right: they showed, through the long day, their ability to represent the monarchy, the modern monarchy, to young people of their generation. Both are extroverts and quick to deflate pretentiousness, especially in themselves.

The new Duchess of York was the star of the pre-wedding interview, another constitutional requirement before royal weddings can be solemnised. She showed how, if she was going to 'obey', her husband was obliged to 'worship'. She showed she was her own person, with her own opinions, and she was respected for that.

Modern royal brides have been married at the Abbey since 1919, when George V gave in to the demands of the rapacious media, needing royal stories for their survival. There have been only two exceptions. The Duke and Duchess of Kent chose York Minster, because, after all, Miss Katherine Worsley was very much from Yorkshire; her roots were there, and the Minster did well by her. The Prince of Wales was enamoured by St Paul's Cathedral, because he wanted a musical wedding, and St Paul's filled the bill. But at this wedding, the old Abbey, bedecked with 30,000 blossoms, looked its best, and came back into the reckoning. The authorities, always suspicious of television, allowed a television camera to take shots from above the altar, and thereby showed to the world what a wedding is about.

On page 104: The newly married Duke and Duchess of York emerge into the sunshine from the Great West Door of Westminster Abbey. The crowds now had a clear view of the bride's face with her veil lifted up and held in place by a diamond tiara, borrowed for the occasion from a friend. The bride's curving bouquet contained many highly scented flowers and was a warm glow of rich creams and ivory.

On page 105: Encouraged by the royal family and cheering crowds below, the Duke of York kisses his bride on the balcony of Buckingham Palace.

The Queen Mother, wearing her favourite combination of pearls and ostrich-feather hat, travelled to the Abbey in an open State Landau with her daughter, Princess Margaret and her two grandchildren, Viscount Linley and Lady Sarah Armstrong-Jones. It is over sixty years since the Queen Mother herself went to the Abbey to marry the Duke of York, George V's second son, and so became the Duchess of York.

All the watching millions saw the new Duke put a ring of Welsh gold on his Duchess's finger – and then, to the mild surprise of the Palace itself, and possibly even of the Archbishop, the couple exchanged rings in public. So all those who had said, sincerely, that they objected to the Duchess agreeing to obey were taken by surprise. It is true that both the Duke of Edinburgh and the Prince of Wales wear wedding rings, but they have done so since their marriages were solemnised. This was the first time that the exchange of rings was seen in public.

What also was plain was that the new Duchess had the charisma to charm crowds, to enlist them on her side and to encourage them to give her the popular support that some of the popular papers had seemed to be denying her. From the moment that the Glass Coach left Clarence House, when the tall, black gates were opened, it was plain to all the world, and its television viewers, that the new Duchess of York was enjoying the day as much as she had enjoyed the four months of the courtship: knowing what the papers were doing, and what they had said about her, but also knowing that the critics, for all their efforts, had become an insubstantial minority. Even for a young woman, out in the world, and reaching the age of twenty-six, the ferocity of some of the criticism of her dress sense, and even of herself, must have been daunting. She knew that the choice of design for her wedding dress would be crucial in the smart world's estimation of her. But she also knew that among plain people, who admired her looks and her independence, the test was going to be if she were true to herself – and so to them. And she was.

The Queen and the Duke of Edinburgh leading the carriage procession from Buckingham Palace, accompanied by a Sovereign's Escort of the Household Cavalry. Wearing an elegant outfit of delphinium blue silk crêpe by Ian Thomas and with dashing organza peonies under the brim of her hat, the Queen looked relaxed and happy on this family occasion.

She dressed herself, and her very young bridesmaids, with fresh flowers in the hair, so that one of her best attributes was not diminished. She showed again that she is an individual: her hair was down, and on her dress and train she ensured that there were embroidered the anchors and waves, the nautical emblems, and the 'A' and 'S' that showed that she meant to tell everyone that her marriage was a love match, and she wished the world to see it that way.

What the wedding day gave to the country, and to the growing world that is still interested in monarchy, was a new person that they could admire and like because it was evident that she liked them. What the Duchess has done is to show that she is her own person, with her own ideas, and with her own forcefulness – and that she is going to be a force in the fashion, and the popularity stakes, for a long time ahead.

There are those who explain the success of the modern monarchy in terms that suggest it is just another soap opera; and it is true that soap operas' best ratings come with a wedding. That may explain some of the foreign, and especially the American, interest. But what the wedding day showed was two people who were setting out on life together without any scriptwriter calling the tune. The world has now learned about the Duke of York and his wife, and has seen how individual they are, how inclined they are to do what they want, and have the self-confidence to believe that they are right to be themselves, and to know that many people will respect their spontaneity. It was pure theatre; the theatre the royal family knows how to do so well, and how to use. And that evening it knew it had a new star in the Duchess of York.

Right: Mrs Nancy Reagan, invited as a friend of the family, waved to the crowd as she arrived at the Abbey.

Below: Princess Anne and Captain Mark Phillips. Their two children had travelled to the Abbey in advance as they were each to be one of the bridesmaids and pages.

Facing page above: The Prince and Princess of Wales travelling in an open State Landau to the Abbey. The Princess of Wales wore a sea-green and black polka-dot dress by Victor Edelstein with a stunning tricorn hat to match.

Facing page below: At 11.05 am precisely the newly created Duke of York left Buckingham Palace with his supporter, Prince Edward in the 1902 State Landau. They were accompanied by a Captain's Escort of the Household Cavalry.

Left: The royal bridegroom wore the ceremonial day dress of a naval lieutenant and his two medals, the South Atlantic Campaign medal and the Jubilee medal. Prince Edward wore the No 1 dress uniform of an acting lieutenant of the Royal Marines.

Below: The happy and relaxed bride waved and smiled her way to the Abbey in the Glass Coach, accompanied by her father, Major Ronald Ferguson. The previous evening Miss Ferguson had told the world in a television interview, 'There will never be a dress to match it'. Her Edwardian-style head-dress of scented flowers kept in position the traditional bridal veil which was beaded throughout with sequins.

Right and below right: Lindka Cierach, designer of the royal wedding dress, rearranging the dress and veil. Made in gleaming ivory silk duchess satin, the dress had a 17½-foot train flowing out from beneath a fan-shaped bow.

Below: Lindka Cierach specializes in delicate embroidery and the beadwork on the wedding dress was scattered with personal themes — the bee emblem was based on the bride's own Coat of Arms.

Centre below: The bride's sequinned veil was made of pure silk bobbinet and scalloped with embroidered hearts along the edge, punctuated with guipure bows.

Far below: The bridesmaids' dresses were made in a soft peach slub taffeta silk, trimmed with ecru and peach cotton lace featuring thistles, bees and bows.

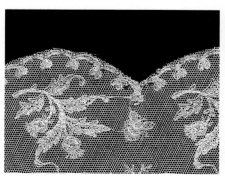

The magnificent wedding service began with the bride and her father processing up the nave of the Abbey to the Sanctuary where the Duke of York was waiting with his supporter, Prince Edward. The bridegroom turned round and gave his bride an encouraging smile as she neared the end of her long walk. The service was conducted by the Archbishop of Canterbury and during the vows there were none of the smiles and giggles that have accompanied the

courtship. They spoke calmly and
confidently and the bride showed no
hesitation over her promise to 'obey'. In
keeping with royal tradition the couple

exchanged rings.
As soon as the newly wed couple
emerged from the Edward the Confessor
Chapel where they signed the register, it

was all smiles again. After the formal
curtsey to the Queen the new Duchess of
York was ready for the final, long
procession down the nave.

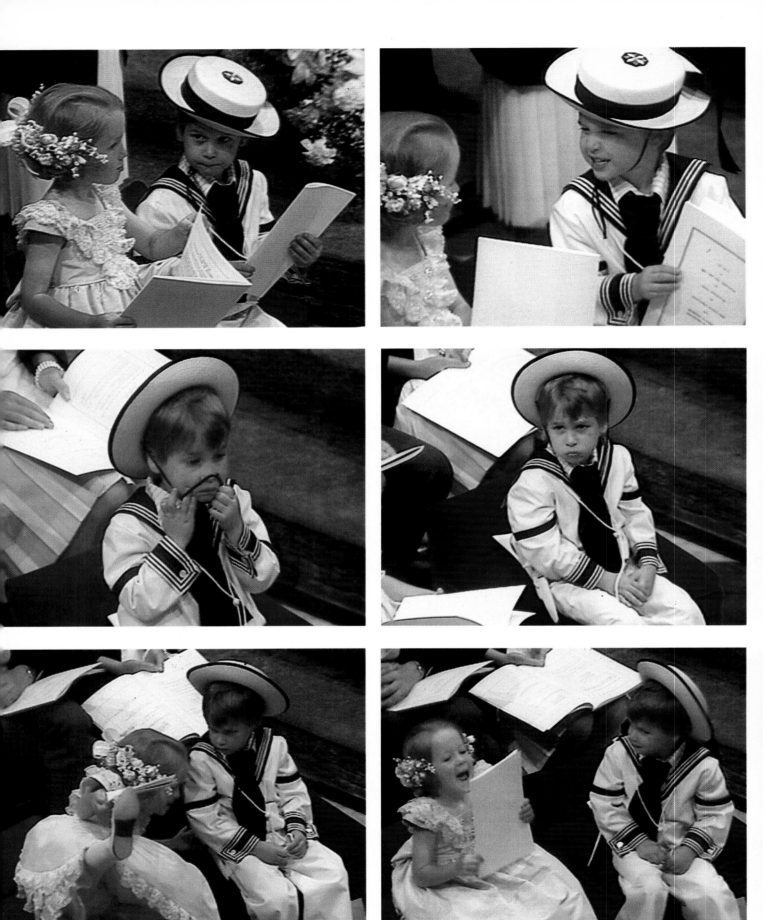

Prince William, aged four, was the youngest of the bride's attendants and during the signing of the register, he and Laura Fellowes, his first cousin, became slightly fidgety.

The two youngest pages wore sailor suits modelled on one worn by Prince Albert Edward, later Edward VII, in 1846 on board the royal yacht. The outfit included a replica, small, white dagger which kept Prince William amused during the long service.

Above left: Alice Ferguson seated next to her brother Andrew, stifles a quick yawn.
Above right: Lady Rosanagh Innes-Ker, as part of her duties as chief bridesmaid,

takes the bride's bouquet at the beginning of the marriage service.
Centre: Alice Ferguson, an attentive bridesmaid, straightens the bride's veil at

the steps of the Sanctuary.
Below: Lady Rosanagh Innes-Ker was accompanied by Peter Phillips, the oldest attendant.

Above left: The Queen wearing her spectacles during the service.
Above right: Major Ferguson in the front with the bride's mother, Mrs Hector Barrantes.

Centre left: The Queen Mother sharing a joke with Prince Philip.
Centre right: Princess Margaret and Captain Mark Phillips.
Below left: The Princess of Wales.

Below right: The Duchess of Gloucester and her daughters.
Facing page: The newly weds passing through Parliament Square on their way back to Buckingham Palace.

Right: The weather was kind to the bridal couple on their return journey to Buckingham Palace and in the sunshine they smiled and waved all the way back from the Abbey. Like the Queen Mother sixty years before her, she was indeed 'the smiling Duchess'.

Below: Prince Edward was in charge of one of the carriages carrying the bride's attendants back from the Abbey, including his high-spirited nephew, Prince William.

Facing page: Prince William and Zara Phillips greeted their Uncle Andrew and his bride on their arrival at the Grand Entrance of Buckingham Palace. The Duchess of York then kissed her attendants in turn before they all went inside the Palace.

SONG FOR THE WEDDING OF
H.R.H. THE PRINCE ANDREW AND MISS SARAH FERGUSON
23 July 1986
by The Poet Laureate, Ted Hughes

THE HONEY BEE AND THE THISTLE

Upon this day in Westminster
That brings the Prince his Bride
Out of the sun there swoops a song
That cannot be denied.

While every television trembles
In the organ blare
And their cardiographs' two butterflies
Are trying to touch in air,

While some weep at the foamy veil
That surges her to bliss
And some drink to the princely hand
That lifts it for the kiss,

Before the Country's dried its eyes
Or bells begin to ring
That Cherub in a shaft of light
Sweetly starts to sing:

When all the birds of Roxburgheshire
  Danced on the lawns, and all
The Salmon of the Tweed cavorted
  Over The Garden Wall
    Gold as the Honey Bee

A Helicopter snatched you up.
  The pilot it was me.
The props, like a roulette wheel,
  Stopped at felicity
    Soft as the Thistle's crown

But now the Abbey columns
  Stand like your ancestors,
And your *I do* has struck a root
  Down through the Abbey floors
    Gold as the Honey Bee

Now like a North pole and a South
  You bear the magnet globe
And axis of our spinning land
  Where chaos plays its strobe
    Soft as the Thistle's crown

But as the day's Commandment
  Which can no longer wait
Yokes Unicorn and Lion both
  To haul the coach of state
    Gold as the Honey Bee

While Royal ghosts in silence
  Bend at the register
And gaze into the letters
  That you have written there
    Soft as the Thistle's crown

Like splitting amplification
  Of thunder come the cheers
And set my meaning humming in
  Your honeymooning ears
    Gold as the Honey Bee

Dance, dance, as Eve and Adam
  Kicked their worries off
In Paradise, before they heard
  God politely cough
    Soft as the Thistle's crown

Then dance on, like a tuning fork
  That wakes unearthly stars
In human hearts, and makes them throb
  Like noble, old guitars
    Gold as the Honey Bee

And dance, and dance, like Sirius
  Inseparably two
Who twirls in heaven, to show the earth
  What harmony can do
    Soft as the Thistle's crown

For from this day, which gives you each
  To each as man and wife
That's the dance, and this the song
  Of a true and happy life
    Gold, gold as the Honey Bee
    Soft as a Thistle's crown

On page 121: The official photographs of the royal wedding were taken in the Throne Room of Buckingham Palace by Albert Watson, an Edinburgh-born fashion photographer who works in New York. On being given the commission, Mr Watson said of the bride, 'I think she is wonderful. I love her hair and her natural beauty; that is something I have to go after.'

Left: The Duke and Duchess of York posing with their families for the official group photograph. Before the wedding Mr Watson described his task: 'My only concern is the time aspect. I shall only have a few minutes to organize everyone.'
Front row, seated (left to right): The Earl of Ulster, Lady Davina Windsor, Lady Rose Windsor, Andrew Ferguson, Lady Rosanagh Innes-Ker, Zara Phillips, Prince William of Wales, Laura Fellowes, Seamus Makim, Alice Ferguson, Peter Phillips, Lady Gabriella Windsor, Lord Frederick Windsor.
Second row: Lady Sarah Armstrong-Jones, Princess Margaret, Princess Anne, the Princess of Wales holding Prince Henry, the Queen Mother, the Queen, the bride and groom, Major Ronald Ferguson, Prince Edward, Mrs Susan Barrantes, Lady Elmhirst, Mrs Jane Makim.
Slightly behind them: the Hon. Mrs Doreen Wright, Major Bryan Wright, Alexander Makim.
Third row: Viscount Linley, Captain Mark Phillips, Marina Ogilvy, the Prince of Wales, Princess Alexandra, the Duke of Edinburgh, Princess Michael of Kent, Princess Alice, the Duchess of Gloucester, the Duchess of Kent, Lady Helen Windsor.
Back row: James Ogilvy, Prince Michael of Kent, the Hon. Angus Ogilvy, the Duke of Gloucester, the Duke of Kent, and the Earl of St Andrews.

The wedding party on the balcony of Buckingham Palace. The bridal couple pretended not to hear the crowd's demands for a kiss and then, much to everyone's delight, the Duke of York gave his new wife a loving kiss. He then helped the Duchess inside with her train and the couple went off to receive the guests.

On pages 126, 127 and 128: The Duke and Duchess of York left Buckingham Palace for their honeymoon in an open State Landau which was decorated with a learner plate and lucky horseshoe, among other things. The Queen, with Prince William, Princess Margaret and many of the Palace staff, gave the couple a resounding send-off, showering them with confetti and 24,000 rose petals to wish them good luck.

ACKNOWLEDGMENTS

The Song by the Poet Laureate, on page 120: © Ted Hughes 1986

The Publishers would particularly like to thank Mauro Carrero for taking the photographs which appear on page 64

The Publishers would also like to thank the following sources:

Alpha Photo: 62 L; (Jim Bennett): 37 AR; (Alan Davidson): 37 AL

British Broadcasting Corporation: 34 BR

Camera Press: 15 A, 16, 17 L, 44, 54-56, 58 A, 87; (Peter Abbey): 94 A, BR; (Cecil Beaton): 18, 88;
(Terence Donovan): frontispiece, 6, 12, 40, 72; (Peter Grugeon): 26; (Glen Harvey): 95; (Patrick Lichfield): 23;
(Norman Parkinson): 91; (Prince Andrew): 35 B, 39 AR; (Gene Nocon): half-title;
(John Scott): 17 R, 19 B, 21, 22 A, 24 CR, AL; (Ian Swift): 7, 11; and (Albert Watson): 121, 122-123

Copyright © College of Arms on pages 41, 73 and 120; Daneshill School, Basingstoke: 57 A

Major Ronald Ferguson: 43, 46-49, 59 A, 60, 61 AL; (Michael Roberts): 59 B

Tim Graham: Front and back jacket, 5, 27 BL, 32 R, 35 A, 36 BR, 37 CR, 45 A, 57 B, 93, 97 BL, 99 B, 100 A, 101 AL,
102 AL, 102 B, 104, 105, 108 B, 109 B, 110 A, 115 AL, 118 B, 119, 124 B, 125 A, 126, 127 A, and 128

Reproduced by gracious permission of Her Majesty the Queen: 75-79

Anwar Hussein: 24 BL, 25, 36 BL, 99 AL, 102 AR, 112 AL, and 127 B

The ILN Picture Library: 15 B, 19 A, 20, 49 BR, 84, 92; (Lisa Sheridan): 9

Independent Television News Limited: 28-29, 106, 109 A, and 125 B

Newspix International (Francis Dias): 37 B, 97 A, and 100 B

Patrick Lichfield: 8; The National Portrait Gallery, London: 74; Desmond O'Neill: 58 B, and 61 AR

Photographers International: 30 A, 36 A, 60 B, 62 AR, 63 L, 65 A, 97 BR, 98, 99 BR, 101 AR, 101 B, 103 AL, 103 AR,
107, and 124 A

Popperfoto: 14, 22 B, 34 A, 83, and 86; Press Association: 33 A, and 65 B

Rex Features: 10, 25 AL, 31, 33 B, 37 CL, 63 AR, 66, 94 BL; (Mauro Carrero): 34 BL, 38, 108 A, 110 B, 111 BR,
117, and 118 A

Ringier (Andy Mettler): 67 B; Ritva Risu, Finland: 50-53; Roxburghe Estate: 68 A; Stare Colour Pictures: 45 B, 63 BR and
103 BL

Syndication International: 24 FB and R, 27 AL, 27 BR, 32 L, 39 L, 67 A, and 71

Thames Television Limited: 69, 111 A, 112-113, 114-115, 116

Topham Picture Library (Cecil Beaton): 13

Picture key: A: Above; AL/R: Above Left/Right; B: Below; BL/R: Below Left/Right; C: Centre;
CL/R: Centre Left/Right; FBL/R: Far Below Left/Right; L: Left; R: Right